Is Hearing Enough?

Literacy and the Great Commandments

Is Hearing Enough?
Literacy and the Great Commandments

Don Edwards

WILLIAM CAREY
LIBRARY

Is Hearing Enough? Literacy and the Great Commandments

Copyright © 2010 by Don Edwards

Unless otherwise noted, all scripture is taken from the HOLY BIBLE, NEW LIVING TRANSLATION®. Copyright © 1996 by Tyndale Charitable Trust. Used by permission of Tyndale House Publishers, Inc. All rights reserved.

Published by William Carey Library
1605 E. Elizabeth Street
Pasadena, CA 91104 | www.missionbooks.org

Rosemary Lee-Norman, editor
Amanda Valloza, graphic design

William Carey Library is a ministry of the
U.S. Center for World Mission
Pasadena, CA | www.uscwm.org

Printed in United States of America

13 12 11 10 09 5 4 3 2 1 CH

Library of Congress Cataloging-in-Publication Data

Edwards, Don.
  Is hearing enough? : literacy and the great commandments / Don Edwards.
    p. cm.
  Includes bibliographical references (p.   ).
  ISBN 978-0-87808-462-3
  1. Literacy--Religious aspects--Christianity. 2. Missions--Educational work--India.
3. Literacy--India. I. Title.
  BV2082.I45C48 2009
  266.00954--dc22

                                    2009027393

Contents

Acknowledgements

Living always involves community. Personal accomplishments can never be separated from the community an individual is a part of. God-given abilities, family upbringing and encouragement, friends, fellow workers, writers that have gone before and educational relationships all are part of any one's achievements. I respectfully thank the community of relationships that have surrounded, challenged and encouraged me through the process of completing this project.

The Word was made flesh and lived among us. With gratefulness to the living Word I give thanks for the privilege for the ability to read the written page and thus to know Him and His will for my life. I thank Dr. Timothy Tennent of Gordon-Conwell Theological Seminary who guided me during the process of thinking through the design and focus of this book.

I also acknowledge and thank Dr. John DeVries, the founder and now retired president of Mission India who encouraged me to pursue doctoral studies in missions. His love for the people of India and passion to see that nation become the crown jewel in our Savior's throne captured my heart and mind over two decades ago. With encouragement from the board of directors and the new president, I was able to commit the necessary time to complete this book. I thank the directors of our program in India, my friends and co-laborers for their continued ministry and emotional support during this process. I also thank the literacy staff for the work done on the research portion of this project. I am grateful for the many friends that prayed with and for me during this time.

Finally, I thank God for His gracious gift to me, my wife. She encouraged and patiently stood with me even while completing her own master's thesis. I also thank my son who assisted me in formulating and analyzing the research data.

Introduction

The emerging church is growing rapidly among the poor, oppressed communities in India. The truth is most of these people are illiterate. Letters and numbers are meaningless symbols. The inability to read and write has a profound debilitating effect on all of life, including spiritual development. As people committed to completing the Great Commission, we need to understand and shape our mission strategies on sound realities.

Church and mission leaders across India have established a target of 20 percent of the Indian population being Christian by the year 2020. This is a net increase of one thousand percent in little more than a decade. The literacy rate in the emerging church currently is low, even among church leaders. With the type of growth proposed, the lack of ability to read the Word of God will have crippling effects on the sustainability of these new believers.

In the pages that follow, my aim is to test the validity of the argument that literacy is important for discipleship. This will be examined from several angles. In chapter 1, we will look at the problems existing for illiterate people. In chapter 2 we will look at the impact illiteracy has on church growth. In chapter 3, we will seek to gain an understanding of what the Bible says about reading and discipleship. Then in chapter 4, we will take a more detailed review of reading in history as it relates to biblical faith. In chapter 5, we will look critically at the Orality Movement. Many believe storytelling and talking Bibles should be the major focus of evangelism and discipleship efforts in developing nations. Without a corresponding emphasis on literacy, Orality's significant contributions will quickly fade. In chapter 6 we will look at literacy as a way to fulfill the Great Compassion. Jesus said we are to love our neighbor as we love ourselves. Literacy is a tangible fulfillment of this command. The human developmental issues related to literacy are indisputable. Chapter 7 will address this.

Looking at the Bible, historical records, and current trends in reaching those who are blind to the written page gives us only a bookish perspective. Limiting our understanding to these factors can result in a seemingly solid theoretical framework with little relationship to the realities in the villages across India. We need to listen to the voices of those planting most of the churches in India to better understand the impact of illiteracy on discipleship. I attempted to do this through surveys and face-to-face interviews. This is the focus of chapter 8.

The first group of leaders surveyed is from the state of Andhra Pradesh. The second group is from across the nation. I tested their observations and perspectives on the relation of literacy to discipleship in two sample groups through face-to-face interviews. The sample groups, one rural and one urban, provide "a logical conceptual framework by which estimates of the characteristics of a population can be inferred from the results of an examination of only a sample of that population."[1]

In the final chapter of this book, we will look at the implications of the importance of literacy upon our evangelism and discipleship efforts.

My goal is to show the Great Commission will be much closer to the Great Completion in India, as well as other developing nations, when missionaries disciple new believers with a Bible in one hand and literacy primers in the other.

---

1   D. J. Casley and D. A. Lury, *Data Collection in Developing Countries* (Oxford: Oxford University Press, 1987), 1.

Chapter 1
The Problems of Illiteracy

The Gospel is better than good news to the poor, oppressed peoples of India. It is *great news!* As large numbers come to Christ, they experience acceptance, forgiveness, value, and freedom like never before. Many of them become followers because of a dramatic encounter with the living God. Disease, demonic control, and addictions often vanish. Jesus Christ becomes to them the only true and living God deserving of their worship and allegiance. From the outset of their decision to follow Christ, many face persecution and are perceived as turning their back on the only community they know. Their zealousness carries them through. Filled with God's Spirit and a story of what God has done, evangelism flows spontaneously.

But there is a crippling problem. Most cannot read the Word of God. In fact, they cannot even write their names. Numbers on currency are meaningless symbols. It is a blindness that stifles the person and their Christian maturity. Surveys conducted for this book estimate a literacy rate among the emerging church in India between 3 and 26 percent. Church leaders face the same predicament. One surprising discovery is that 69 percent of the leadership in the new congregations is illiterate. That means fewer than one out of three leaders in the emerging churches can read the Bible. Therefore, more than two-thirds of those leaders have no way to feed themselves and therefore no reliable way to feed the people they shepherd. And yet their faith is vibrant, yet short on access to the truth—it is a precarious beginning.

Illiteracy in the church results in stunted growth. But it does not have to be this way. Literacy is a useful tool for discipling those in the emerging church in India. For without it, immaturity, stunted growth, heresy and reconversion back into Hinduism will continue. And this statement does not even account for the ongoing dehumanizing impact of illiteracy on human development.

The goal of this book is to demonstrate that illiteracy hinders discipleship in the emerging church in India.

A Place to Start

The church in India is rapidly growing among the poor, oppressed communities in India. Illiteracy plagues these people. This plague is nondiscriminatory. It affects Hindus, Muslims and Christians alike. During the research for this book, we found distinct behavioral differences between literate and nonliterate believers. Of course there are exceptions, but a meaningful comparison is possible. A literate membership is not *essential* but *beneficial* to the church at large. Taking this one step further, it is possible to assert that a literate leadership of the emerging church is *essential* and not just *beneficial*. An oral Bible is not enough. The Orality Movement, though correctly emphasizing teaching methodologies to reach the world's illiterates, does not adequately address the implications of illiteracy on all of life. This means orality alone will leave the mushrooming church crippled and unable to sustain itself.

Key Questions on Literacy and Spiritual Growth

The key questions addressed in this book include:

- Does literacy really matter?
- Has not the church survived and, in fact, spread during the last two millenniums without widespread literacy?
- Did not the low rate of literacy before, during, and after the time of Christ have little or no impact on the growth and discipleship of the early followers of Jesus Christ?
- Has illiteracy affected the church throughout history?
- Do not illiterates have a better memory than those exposed to writing and are therefore better able to retain the spoken Word in their hearts and minds?

In this first chapter, we will examine the crippling problems created by illiteracy on all facets of life. In the following chapters, we will look at the useful role literacy plays in bringing the whole Gospel to the whole person and its strategic use in discipling this nation.

The Setting: Crippling Problems of Illiteracy

"The most bruised people on this planet, the naked, the hungry, the fallen among thieves, the sick, the imprisoned in mind and soul . . . almost every illiterate is in debt all his life—and his children and his children's children after him. He does not know how much his debt is, or whether the interest is correct. The moneylender takes all he can and still keeps his victim alive—for it would be silly to kill the animal that makes him rich. In one form or another, this is the black sorrow of nearly every illiterate in the world."[2] And according to *India Today*, "Half of the world's illiterates live in India."[3] Even the most conservative estimates by the government of India in the 2001 census reveal more illiterates in India than the total population of the United States of America.[4]

The research among the emerging church reveals significantly lower percentages of literates than a casual view of the 2001 India census. One of the primary reasons for this difference is that the church is growing primarily among the poor outcasts of society. In chapter 8 of this book, K.S. Singh's work is cited for the control groups studied. The 1981 census data reveals a 7.77 percent and 16.94 percent literacy rate among these two people groups. This literacy rate is consistent with estimates made by church planters and mission leaders surveyed for this book.

Illiteracy and Oppression

An illustration of the "black sorrow" of illiteracy is from a shameful time in American history, when the nation was guilty of exploiting black Africans as slaves. In the book entitled *Narrative of the Life of Fredrick Douglass, An American Slave*, Douglass quotes one of his owners:

> If you give a nigger an inch, he will take an ell [45 inches]. A nigger should know nothing but to obey his master—to do as he is told to do. Learning will spoil the best nigger in the world. Now if you teach that nigger (speaking of myself) how to read, there would be no keeping him. It would forever unfit him to be a slave. He would at once become unmanageable and of no value to his master. As to himself, it could do him no good, but a great deal of harm.

---

2   Frank C. Laubach, *The Silent Billion Speak* (New York: Friendship Press, 1945), 1–2.

3   Shankkar Aiyar, "India's Worst," *India Today*, 25 August 2003, 24–26.

4   India Census Data, 2001, http://www.censusindia.net/t_00_006.html. The census indicates the number of literates in India is 560,687,797 and this is 64.84% of the total. The total population considered as potentially literate is 864,790,714. This leaves a balance of 304,102,917 illiterates in India as of 2001. The population of the US in 2001 was 278,058,881.

It would make him discontented and unhappy.[5]

These were the words of Mr. Auld, the slaveowner, to his wife when he discovered she was teaching young Frederick Douglass to read. She had taken too kindly to this slave boy and he wanted to put an immediate stop to this destructive learning. Later on in his life Douglass reflected:

> I have found that, to make a contented slave, it is necessary to make a thoughtless one. It is necessary to darken his moral and mental vision, and, as far as possible, to annihilate the power of reason. He must be able to detect no inconsistencies in slavery; he must be made to feel that slavery is right. And he can be brought to that only when he ceases to be a man.[6]

What was it the slaveowner feared? What is it the moneylender and landlord fear today in India? A person who understands he is a human being, someone created in the image of God. For a person who is whole resists exploitation and oppression and stands up for their fundamental human rights.

Another example of the threat literacy poses to the oppressors is the slave revolt in Bahia, Brazil in 1835. "So worried did the authorities become about the power of the book in the hands of the slaves that those who could read and write were packed off back to West Africa, leaving behind the illiterates, who were less likely to engage in an effective struggle."[7] Illiteracy is the means by which the powerful control the powerless to maintain their dominion.

The two illustrations above identify clearly the oppression that so often accompanies and institutionalizes illiteracy. But its devastation is much broader. The person's health and finances suffer because of their inability to read the written page. Illiteracy is the greatest threat to the development of Africa. "Illiteracy affects the capacity of ordinary poor people to earn a decent livelihood and experience human dignity, it exacerbates the spread of HIV/AIDS, locks individuals and whole

---

5   Frederick Douglass, *Narrative of the Life of Frederick Douglass, an American Slave* (New York: Penguin Putnam, Inc., 1997), 47.

6   Ibid., 102.

7   Jack Goody, *The Power of the Written Tradition* (Washington & London: Smithsonian Institution Press, 2000), 164–165.

communities into spiraling poverty, and it threatens our capacity to engage in an ever-globalizing social, economic, and political world" says Charles Abani, country director of Action Aid Nigeria.[8] According to USAID, illiteracy contributes to high mortality rates among infants, more deaths in childbirth, sickly children, and out of control birthrates.

Literacy is a critical need because illiteracy not only cripples the individual, but the nation. Kofi A. Annan, in the foreword to the 1999 UNICEF annual report, says, "Education is a human right with immense power to transform. On its foundation rest the cornerstones of freedom, democracy, and sustainable human development."[9] This statement is an invitation to the 'love' vision of the church. "At the same time, the consequences of illiteracy are profound, even potentially life threatening. They flow from the denial of a fundamental human right: the right to education, proclaimed in agreements ranging from the 50-year-old Universal Declaration of Human Rights to the 1989 Convention on the Rights of the Child, the world's most embraced human rights instrument."[10]

In 2000, the United Nations adopted a millennium declaration with a focus on eight Millennium Development Goals. They are:

1. Eradicate extreme poverty.
2. Achieve universal primary education.
3. Promote gender equality.
4. Reduce child mortality.
5. Improve maternal health.
6. Combat HIV/AIDS.
7. Ensure environmental sustainability.
8. Develop a global partnership for development.[11]

"Literacy is at the heart of UNESCO's mandate."[12] "Faced with the gap between literates and illiterates in terms of social, civic, and economic

8   Donald Andoor, "Group Identifies Illiteracy as Threat to Africa's Development," *This Day*, 24 January 2002.

9   Carol Bellamy, *The State of the World's Children 1999* (Education: United Nations Children's Fund, 1999), 4.

10   Ibid., 7.

11   UNESCO, *Millennium Development Goals (MDGs)* 2005, http:portal.unesco.org/education;en;ev.php-URL_ID=41138&URL_DO=DO_TOPIC&U.

12   *United Nations Literacy Decade (UNLD) and LIFE*, 2005, http:portal.unesco.org/education;en;ev.php-URL_ID=41139&URL_DO=DO_TOPIC&U.

opportunities, UNESCO focuses its efforts toward achieving literacy for all...."[13] In their international plan for action for the United Nations, the number one objective is to place literacy "at the centre of national education systems and development efforts."[14] Those of us involved in Christian mission efforts among illiterate peoples must not ignore the devastating effects of illiteracy on all of life.

A Case Study: Illiteracy in India

The government of India has the stated goal of making their nation a literate nation. This is quite a task given the fact that, "as far as India is concerned, mass illiteracy continues and this biggest democracy can today only boast of harboring the largest number of illiterates in the world."[15]

> At the dawn of independence,
> We made a tryst with destiny,
> To liberate our illiterate masses from the thralldom of ignorance.
> Even after 54 years of independence,
> Even after nine five-year plans,
> Have we achieved this?
> The answer is an emphatic "No."
> In fact, the number of illiterates has gone up.
> Why is it so?
> What prevented us from achieving our goal?
> Did we make sincere efforts?
> Did we stick to our goals?[16]

It is important for us to listen to the cry of the nation.

From a nation-building perspective, even at a level of global security, literacy is primary. But there are opponents. Ashok Singhal is a leader among the Hindu nationalist movements, the Vishwa Hindu Parishad. Dilip D'Souza says:

---

13   *UNESCO and Literacy: Strategy,* 2005, http:portal.unesco.org/education;en;ev.php-URL_ID=41145&URL_DO=DO_TOPIC&U.
14   Ibid.
15   G. Sivaswamy, "Top Priority Needed for Eradicating Illiteracy," *The Hindu,* September, 11 2001.
16   Ibid.

He (Singhal) cannot really stand the idea of ending illiteracy in India . . . imagine how the prospect terrifies him. The more India's masses get educated, aware, the more we will start asking questions. We will ask questions about our condition: about the dirt, injustice, hunger, corruption, thirst, disease, and oppression that lie everywhere. We will ask questions about Singhal's rhetoric about temples and conspiracies and spreading radioactive sand around the country: rhetoric that was deliberately designed for an essentially unquestioning audience. We will want to know exactly what this rhetoric has to do with any of the daily problems in our lives. . . . The thought of facing such questions frightens him. That is why he really wants us Indians to remain largely illiterate.[17]

The opposition to literacy is fundamentally religious and motivated by power. As people seek education, the blinders that keep them enslaved by the oppressive caste system begin to diminish. Light fills the mind and truth exposes the lies and deception of a religious system established to support the rule of the Brahmin. It is because of this that the government's nine five-year plans to eradicate literacy have failed. It is because of this that warehouses of literacy primers never empty. The Hindutva leadership fear the knowledge of the masses, and so they give instructions to not distribute the tools to transform the nation.

In spite of opposition to literacy, the census data indicates a steep rise in the literacy rates in India. However, literacy efforts are actually thwarted through distorted reporting of national census data. In 1991, the Indian census reports that 52.2 percent of the population was literate.[18] The 2001 census now indicates an increase of 13.18 percent to 65.38 percent literate.[19] However, many claim this is false.

For over a century now, literacy, as defined for the country's census data collecting agencies, is no more than the "ability to read and write a simple letter." This is from 1981 to 1991, when the last census was conducted. "We have made no progress in our understanding or definition of what it means to be lettered. And even in this limited definition,

---

17   Dilip D'Souza, "Of White Powders and other Benefits," *Rediff,* 6 January 1999.
18   Census of India 1991, "Part IVA—Social and Cultural Tables."
19   Census of India 2001, "Provisional Population Totals: India," Paper 1.

we've failed. No tests are conducted by data collectors during surveys. People are merely asked whether they are literate or not and entries are made."[20]

What is the motivation for overstating the literacy rate? There are two reasons. First, it is an international image issue. India's political leaders do not want the position of being at the head of the world's most illiterate nation. Second, it is a power issue. If we can claim the eradication of illiteracy, then the need for continued literacy training goes away and a substantial part of the Indian population remains uneducated and subservient to the upper caste elite.

The sinful passions of the powerful should not hinder obedience to Jesus' call to bring freedom to the captives. Our own brothers and sisters in Christ remain shackled in illiteracy. A discipling vision includes setting captives free. Jesus did not let the powerful intimidate him. Nor did he start a violent revolution. In Matthew 12:18–20 we read that "he will proclaim *justice* to the nations. He will not fight or shout; he will not raise his voice in public. He will not crush those who are weak, or quench the smallest hope, until he brings full *justice* with his final victory. And his name will be the hope of all the world." Literacy is a useful part in ushering in the justice of the King.

Implications

The first to respond to the Gospel message are the poor. And in most cases, the world over, the condition of poverty stems from the inability to read. It is important for Great Commission ministries to engage in tackling root problems that have plagued humanity for centuries. This is a matter of biblical justice with the opportunity to bring spiritual transformation at the same time.

---

20   Soma Wadhwa, "When Numbers Lie," *Outlook India*, April, 9 2002.

Chapter 2
Illiteracy and Church Growth

A report by a group of mission organizations working in North India summarized the number of new churches planted in recent years. During a 28-month period, over 58,000 new gatherings of believers were established. This seems nothing short of miraculous. God's Spirit is moving across India today! In looking at previous reports submitted by this group, the average number of new believers per gathering is 10. This is wonderful news. But the progress this information appears to indicate in our goal of completing the Great Commission is limited. The tremendous growth seen still only nets an additional 250,000 new believers per year in North India. In order for the church in India to *maintain* its current percent of the national population, it needs to grow at twice that rate. In the apparent rapid spread of the Gospel in India today, the church, even though growing numerically, is just maintaining its current percentage of the population.

The story of one missionary couple illustrates the important role of literacy in the discipleship process. Perhaps it reveals one of the keys to unlocking the mystery as to why Christianity remains stagnate as far as a percentage of India's population. Samuel and his wife Hepzibah (names are changed), a missionary couple from Tamil Nadu, are working among the Bhil tribe in Rajasthan and Gujarat. There has been an incredible response to the Gospel. The Bhils are the second largest scheduled tribe of India with over 7.3 million members.[21] They are a violent, untrusting society with bows and arrows sold like vegetables in the marketplace. They are not hunters, however, and use these items to steal, fight, and protect themselves.

This couple's ministry started just over 15 years ago, when their third daughter was born. On June 21, 1991, they celebrated her birth. Three days later they mourned her death. Five days later they found a

---

21   K.S. Singh, *The Scheduled Tribes, People of India National Series,* Volume III, (Delhi: Oxford University Press, 1994), 118.

building to live in so they could stay and work among the Bhil people. The house was available because no one else dared to cross the threshold. Occupied by demons, the villagers said that any who entered it would die. In spite of the great loss of their daughter and the reputation of their new residence, they officially began their ministry on July 1, 1991. The Bhils were yet to hear of the love of Christ.

The third day after moving into their spirit-infested home (now cleansed), both Samuel and Hepzibah saw Jesus in a vision. To them it was more than a vision. They said Jesus actually stood before them in the night. He told them this is where he wanted them. He said the death of their daughter was the seed in the ground that would result in a great harvest.

They began their ministry, as so many others in India—with prayer. On Fridays they would invite people for prayer gatherings at which they would anoint the sick and needy with coconut oil. Often they would go through a liter of oil in an evening, praying for as many as 400 people individually.

When they were introduced to a grass-roots church planting strategy, significant church growth and leadership development began in 1996-1997. They had four on-site classes and a total of 48 students. Today they have 405 evangelists with a total of 620 worshipping groups and approximately 86,000 baptized believers. Each of these groups has a minimum of ten families and some have as many as 150. All of this occurred in the last decade and a half.

Today there are more than 180 church buildings; all funded through churches and Bible study groups in Tamil Nadu. None of these buildings were funded from abroad. In addition, their 405 full time workers are also funded through these same groups in Tamil Nadu. He said that approximately 90 percent of their funding is from within India and only 10 percent from abroad.

Miracles have been a core element in the responsiveness of the Bhils. "Every month, 100 miracles happen. During April of 2003, three people were raised from the dead," said Samuel. Last year alone, their children's ministry, similar to a Vacation Bible School program, reached 30,000 Bhil children.

One of the great challenges of this ministry is that virtually all Bhils are illiterate. People embrace the Gospel, but without the ability to read, they remain steeped in superstition with no means for spiritual nourishment. *This has resulted in only a 10 percent retention rate of new believers, and even they cannot understand much of the teaching.*

In addition, the leadership has a very small knowledge base. Lack of literacy, according to Samuel, is crippling.

From their perspective, literacy is absolutely critical. Literacy elevates people to become leaders in their communities. They become aware of their basic needs. Parents begin to see the importance of sending their children to school. And they say that at a minimum, at least the elders in each congregation should be literate. Currently they have 3,200 elders, of which 90 percent can now read, thanks to the teaching of a literacy program in this tribal area.

"It is a remarkable fact that in 200 years, when India was under British rule, the Christian population of India never exceeded 3 percent of the population."[22] Even today the census reveals virtually no growth. This is in sharp contrast to South Korea. At the turn of the twentieth century, South Korea was 0.5 percent Christian. By the end, 41 percent of their people claim to be followers of Jesus Christ.[23] One of the major differences between South Korea and India is that the Koreans were a literate people. Those coming to Christ could read the Bible for themselves and learn by those who could speak from the written Word. Small groups of believers would meet regularly to study the Bible together. This cannot happen in the majority of new churches blossoming across India today. Could it be that one of the main reasons church growth has remained stagnant for generations, if not for centuries, is the neglect of the critical importance of literacy in the discipling process?

As a nation, India expands by approximately 20 million people per year. The church needs to have a net growth rate of approximately 500,000 new converts per year simply to maintain 2.3 percent of the population.

An important consideration in the preparation of this book is not only the current setting in India, but national plans for the future. "Bless India" was launched in 2005. The vision of this initiative is "to evangelize and disciple by 2020 all the people groups of India by providing mature transformational leadership toward Vision 2020 (20 percent India Christian by 2020)."[24] The target is to see India become

---

22   Vinay Lal, "Anti-Christian Violence in India," http://www.sscnet.ucla.edu/southasia/index.html.

23   David B. Barrett, *World Christian Encyclopedia*, Volume 1 (New York: Oxford University Press, 2001), 682.

24   Emil Jebasing, "Summary of the Proposals of the Follow-up Committee that met on

20 percent Christian by the year 2020. The conference convened in January of 2006 bringing 500 mission organizations together to focus on this objective. Looking at church growth throughout history, there has never been a comparable movement to Christ in terms of its shear mass. Nonetheless, a goal such as this can and does challenge ministries to evaluate strategies and make adjustments to plan for and accommodate substantial growth.

Using percentages extrapolated from the *Statistical Outline of India 2004–2005*, the Christian population in India as of January 2006 was 26 million.[25] (David Bennett, in *The World Christian Encyclopedia*, states the percentage of Christians in India at 6.2 percent.[26] I have chosen to use the government census rate of 2.3 percent). According to the last president of India, A. P. J. Abdul Kalam, "India's population is projected at 1.3 billion by the year 2020."[27] The 20 percent target established by the Bless India committee therefore has a target of 260 million Christians in India by the year 2020. This is a net growth of 234 million new Christians in little more than a decade. This will require an annual growth rate of 17.6 percent, averaging 15.6 million new converts per year for 15 years. Even though this seems improbable, it is a target mission organizations and churches can pray and work towards. The mission statement of this gathering is descriptive of how this target will become a focus:

> To identify and bring together churches and missions committed to the Great Commission task and enable them to work together with strategic plans to develop qualitative (that protects standards of excellence and upholds biblical values) leadership that results in healthy, reproducing, discipling churches in all geographical units within the different people and social groups in India, with measurable goals towards Vision 2020.[28]

In the process of striving toward this objective, does literacy have

---

27 Oct 2005." *BLESS India Gathering and Every Tongue & Tribe Conference.*

25   Roy Siddhartha and R. G. Katoti, eds. *Statistical Outline of India 2004–2005* (Mumbai: Tata Services Limited, 2005), 32.

26   David B. Barrett, 680.

27   A. P. J. Abdul Kalam, *India 2020: A Vision for the New Millennium* (New Delhi: Penguin Books India, 2002), 62.

28   Jebasing.

a role? Today, according to the research done for this book, nearly 70 percent of the emerging churches have illiterate leaders shepherding congregations. If the church were to expand by 236 million in a little more than a decade, this would mean approximately 3.3 million new churches, assuming an average of 70 people per congregation. In India today, a typical pastor shepherds three congregations, so the minimum demand for new leadership is at least 1.1 million new leaders and teachers. Literate leadership is a critical need of the church in the coming years. A literate membership will stabilize and strengthen a rapidly growing movement across India.

Implications

In looking at the developing world, where most of the unreached peoples live, it is wise to consider the social conditions that restrict the growth of the church. Broadcast and print media are wonder tools, but leave unaddressed conditions which restrict discipleship and sustained growth vital to completing the task.

In the next chapter we will explore the important link between literacy and discipleship.

Chapter 3
Literacy and Discipleship

The position that literacy is a useful tool in the discipling of the emerging church in India is based on several theological principles. First, God's Word as revealed and recorded in the Bible is necessary for discipleship. If indeed the written Word is necessary, is not the ability to read the written page important for discipleship?

There is also a direct relationship between literacy and the Great Commandment, to love my neighbor as I love myself. Acknowledging that some level of discipleship does occur among the illiterate, is it not the loving responsibility of the church to elevate these brothers and sisters so they no longer have to live a life under the oppressive bonds of untouchability and absolute poverty?

Many congregations exist across India where many of the believers have a Bible in their own language, carry it to church, sleep with it on their chest as protection against the evil one, but have no ability to read even one word from its pages. It is simply not enough to place Bibles in the hands of new believers who cannot read them. Without the ability to read, the Bible is not much different from an amulet syncretized from their not so former Hindu life, a sophisticated Christian good luck charm.

But before examining these issues, we need to ask, "What is a disciple?"

Discipleship
Dietrich Bonhoeffer, in his classic book *The Cost of Discipleship*, begins his chapter on "The Call to Discipleship" with Mark 2:14, "As he walked along, he saw Levi, son of Alphaeus, sitting at his tax collection booth. 'Come, be my disciple,' Jesus said to him. So Levi got up and followed him." Bonhoeffer then says, "The call goes forth, and is at once followed by the response of obedience."[29] The disciple is not one who simply makes a confession of faith, but acts in obedience to Christ's

---

29   Dietrich Bonhoeffer, *The Cost of Discipleship* (New York: Macmillan, 1967), 61.

call. Bonhoeffer then asks why it is that we are not told if there is some time lag between Christ's call and Levi's obedience. Surely, something must have happened between the two events linked so closely in this verse. Perhaps the tax collector knew Jesus before and his previous acquaintance helps us understand why he dropped everything to follow Jesus. But the text is "ruthlessly silent on this point, and in fact, it regards the immediate sequence of call and response as a matter of crucial importance."[30] No reason is given; he simply obeys Jesus. "We are not expected to contemplate the disciple, but only him who calls, and his absolute authority. According to our text, there is no road to faith or discipleship, no other road—only obedience to the call of Jesus."[31]

The Great Commission and Discipleship

Matthew 28:19–20 is the cornerstone text for this section. "Therefore, go and make disciples of all nations, baptizing them in the name of the Father and the Son and the Holy Spirit. Teach these new disciples to obey all the commands I have given you. And be sure of this: I am with you always, even to the end of the age." How do we go about obeying Christ's command to "make disciples"? The Great Commission is not about making converts, but disciples who obey the call of Jesus as Bonhoeffer has said. Who and what are disciples of Jesus Christ? Does the Great Commission really call for radical obedience? Here we will examine the discipling portion of the verses, the historical setting of Jewish discipleship, and then contrast it with what I believe Jesus is calling us to make "in our going." In this process, we will attempt to understand the impact literacy has on discipleship.

What is it Jesus emphasizes in perhaps the last words he shared with his disciples before he ascended to heaven? It is not that our primary call is to go into the entire world. Not really. This is assumed. "The structure of the passage indicates the major emphasis of the commission, which lies in the aorist imperative ("make disciples"), which is complemented by an aorist participle ("go"), which is also part of the command. The present participles indicate how the making of disciples is to be carried out."[32] "In the Greek, 'go'—like 'baptizing' and 'teaching'—is a participle. Only the verb 'make disciples' is imperative. . . . The main emphasis,

30   Ibid., 61.
31   Ibid., 62.
32   Cleon L. Rogers, "The Great Commission," *Bibliotheca sacra*, July–September 1973, 262.

then, is on the command to 'make disciples,' which in Greek is one word, *matheteusate*, normally an intransitive verb, here used transitively. ... Disciples are those who hear, understand, and obey Jesus' teaching."[33] Literally, the original text says, "Having gone, therefore make disciples . ..."[34] "Make disciples" is by itself an imperative. It is a brisk command, an order. Baptism and obedience to Christ's commands is an integral part of the process of disciple making.

Discipleship in History

"Throughout history, one of the chief motors of literacy has been religion."[35]Literacy has been critical to the Jewish and Christian faith. According to Steven Fischer in his excellent *History of Reading*, he states, "Because writing is such an effective medium of arresting, preserving and conveying sacred knowledge, able to safeguard verbatim the extended teachings of venerated personalities without human oral mediation, reading and writing of religious literature began to play an even more salient role in society."[36] For the Jews, "the written word in fact became fundamental to the Jewish identity. After dedication to God, learning (the reading and interpreting of 'sacred' texts) is the Jew's next duty to his faith."[37] Christianity, from its roots, is known as a faith of the Book. It is grounded in the pages of Scriptures. Discipleship without the Bible is difficult to imagine.

Discipleship was not a concept originated by Jesus. In Greek history, it is used in several ways: First, *manthano* (the Greek word used for disciple) denotes the process by which one acquires theoretical knowledge. ... Socrates held that, when a man is learning something, he should penetrate deeply into the nature of everything. He should be able to proceed beyond this "insight" to a knowledge of morality so as to be able to act according to ethical principles. Second, a man is called a *mathētēs* when he binds himself to someone else in order to acquire his practical and theoretical knowledge. He may be an apprentice in a trade, a student of medicine, or a member of a philosophical school. One can only be a *mathētēs* in the company of a *didaskalos*, a master or

---

33   Frank E. Gaebelein, editor, *The Expositor's Bible Commentary, Volume 8* (Grand Rapids: Zondervan, 1984), 595–596.

34   William Hendriksen, *New Testament Commentary, Exposition of the Gospel According to Matthew* (Grand Rapids: Baker, 1979), 999.

35   Steven Roger Fischer, *A History of Reading* (London: Reaktion Books, 2003), 40.

36   Ibid., 41.

37   Ibid., 61.

teacher, to whom the *mathētēs*, since the days of the sophists, generally
had to pay a fee.[38]

In the Old Testament, the concept of *manthanō*, often equated with
learning, is clear in Deuteronomy,

> where Israel is in great danger of forgetting Yahweh's goodness,
> of taking no further notice of Yahweh's will and of forfeiting its
> election and the divine promises of salvation (cf. Deut. 6:10–12;
> 8:17; 9:4–6; 11:2). Israel must now learn to obey and perform
> the revealed will of God (Deut. 4:10; 14:23; 17:19; 31:12 f.). In
> each of these cases, the object of *manthanō* is ... to fear the Lord
> God. Learning means the process by which the past experience
> of the love of God is translated by the learners into obedience to
> the Torah of God (cf. Deut. 4:14). It means fully understanding
> the Torah, which in Deuteronomy is the whole story of the
> saving actions of God's will. This understanding is to lead to an
> inner acceptance of the divine will (cf. Deut. 30:14).[39]

Mathētēs has much less textual support and is found only in the
LXX in alternative readings.

> The lack of any OT vocabulary for a learner, such as the
> teacher-pupil relationship describes, is bound up with Israel's
> consciousness of being an elect people. This excludes any
> possibility of a disciple-master relationship between men,
> because even the priest and the prophet do not teach on their
> own authority. There is no place for the establishment of a
> master-disciple relationship, nor is there the possibility of
> setting up a human word alongside the Word of God which
> is proclaimed, nor of trying to ensure the force of the divine
> address by basing it on the authority of a great personality.[40]

However, an understanding of discipleship in Rabbinic Judaism
is not the same. "Discipleship, at its foundation, is a social system that
binds at least two persons (but normally more) into a specific hierarchical

---

38   Colin Brown, editor, *The New International Dictionary of New Testament Theology*,
      Volume 1, (Grand Rapids: Zondervan, 1979), 483–484.
39   Ibid., 484.
40   Ibid., 485.

relationship. A central transaction in that relationship is the transmission of culturally privileged knowledge from the superior to the subordinate."[41] It is more than is normally present in family relationships. "In the disciple-community the disciple returns to the psychological situation of childhood to be fundamentally re-formed as a human being. Whereas the child is formed through emulation of the adult kin, the disciple's task of emulation involves absorbing the teaching of the master in such a way as to embody the master's own human achievement."[42] What is it that the master has achieved? He "has reached that form of human perfection held out by tradition as the highest attainable.... The master can displace the biological parents in the disciples' scale of loyalties and affections."[43] Discipleship is caught as well as taught, but fundamental to the transmission of values and behavior is the ability to know the truth. Literacy is crucial at this point.

According to Jaffee, "The discipleship community is a setting for the transmission of transformative knowledge in which the emulation of the imparter of knowledge is both a primary goal of knowledge and proof of its possession."[44] The transmission of knowledge that transforms is at the heart of discipleship. From a literacy perspective, it is important to note that "texts of all sorts constitute the *principle* medium of the exchange of transformative knowledge. The master is the master because of a perceived capacity to impart the essential meaning of such texts: the disciple is defined by the thirst for the knowledge they contain and the will to submit to their norms" (emphasis mine).[45] Texts can be orally transmitted, but they always begin with texts, not just oral truth seemingly remembered verbatim. As demonstrated later in chapter 5, nonliterate learners do not have the capacity of verbatim memory.

With these comments, we can appreciate the discipline of Rabbis and their disciples in memorizing vast amounts of scriptural texts. The written word is the basis of the memorization and it required tremendous discipline and time to accomplish this task.

"While the Written Torah was undoubtedly read aloud, studied, and interpreted as a document, it was also . . . a text that was carried in the memory. The master of the scriptural text testifies to a comprehensive

---

41   Martin S. Jaffee, "A Rabbinic Ontology of the Written and Spoken Word: On Discipleship, Transformative Knowledge, and the Living Texts of Oral Torah," *Journal of the American Academy of Religion*, Fall 1967: 529.

42   Ibid., 530.

43   Ibid., 530.

44   Ibid., 531.

45   Ibid., 531.

project of memorization that yielded a Scripture known backwards and forwards, inside out, and upside down."[46] "The Written Torah was an oral as much as a written text."[47] People memorized it so it would become a part of their soul, while grounded in unchanging written truth.

Definition of Discipleship

Discipleship begins with evangelism. Many in India today are resistant to overt evangelistic efforts. Literacy is an effective door opener to such communities. God called V. David (name changed) through a vision to bring the Gospel to a primitive tribal group who lived between two hills. It was several years later while traveling in a border area between Andhra Pradesh and Chhattisgarh that he saw before him the exact two hills God had shown him in the vision. David knew this was the place he was to go, so he immediately set off through the jungle to the spot between these two hills.

The distance from the nearest road was 12 miles through the forest. When he got to the spot he thought was consistent with the vision, he discovered, to his amazement, a primitive people with loin clothes, no tops, no currency, and bamboo bows and arrows. They were a tribal group called the Koyas. God had been faithful. As he began to communicate the love of God in Jesus to them, they became furious. They demanded he immediately leave. They had their own gods and goddesses and did not want to anger them. They threatened David's life if he did not flee.

He refused discouragement. After a short interlude, he again made the long trek back to the village and again fled under a death threat. This happened a total of three times. His faith was severely tested. He questioned God. "Why have you called me to a people who want nothing to do with me? Please show me what to do or I will have to give up." It was then that he was introduced to the idea of teaching literacy as a door opener for discipleship.

He returned to the village and instead of immediately preaching, he asked them if they would like to learn to read. Their response was, "Here is a hut in which you can live." He then asked, "What am I going to eat?" and they said, "We will give you a tenth of all we kill in the forest." Just a few short years later, there are now over 5,000 baptized believers and a number of churches established.

---

46   Ibid., 535.
47   Ibid., 536.

Literacy opens the door to discipleship, but discipleship is more than evangelism. What did Jesus mean by "disciple"? Just as the rabbinic disciples strove to become like their teacher, "in the Gospels, discipleship (the process of becoming like Christ) was accomplished by being physically with Christ, seeing what He did, hearing what He said, being corrected by Him, and following His example."[48] One can argue the point here purposely excludes the ability to read what Jesus said. Jesus was the Word made flesh. His presence revealed the Father. Without his presence it is reckless to assume that the ability to read the Word of God is not useful in knowing and understanding the truth.

First, discipleship is a call to lay down one's life. A disciple is not a person who simply makes a verbal assent to accept Christ as their personal Savior. Discipleship does have a beginning point. Like the twelve disciples, this point is the call of God on their lives. When Jesus said "make disciples" he was not referring to easy believism. Jesus is very clear. In Luke 14:26-28, Jesus says, "If you want to be my follower, you must love me more than your own father and mother, wife and children, brothers and sisters—yes, more than your own life. Otherwise, you cannot be my disciple. And you cannot be my disciple if you do not carry your own cross and follow me. But don't begin until you count the cost." Then Jesus reiterates his point in verse 33, "So no one can become my disciple without giving up everything for me." Jesus' call to discipleship is to love God and others. "It is unthinkable to divorce the Christian life of love and justice from being a disciple. Discipleship involves a commitment to God's reign, to justice and love, and to obedience to the entire will of God. . . . To become a disciple means a decisive and irrevocable turning to both God and neighbor."[49]

In thinking of this type of radical commitment, it is important to reflect on what is most important. The religious leader concerned about this very question, asked Jesus in Mark 12:28, "Of all the commandments, which is the most important?" Jesus then summarized it all with loving God and loving your neighbor. Scot McKnight, in his article on the Jesus Creed, summarizes it this way: "Discipleship is not so much about radical commitment as it is about radical love, and the disciplines are not so much about spiritual formation as about love

---

48   James G. Samra, "A Biblical View of Discipleship," *Bibliotheca sacra*, April–June 2003, 222.

49   David J. Bosch, *Transforming Mission: Paradigm Shifts in Theology of Mission* (New York: Orbis Books, 2000), 81–82.

formation. . . . The true indicator of spiritual well-being is growth in the ability to love God and people."[50]

Second, discipleship is a call to truth. Jesus identified himself as the truth (John 14:6) and said the truth will set us free (John 8:32). In Deuteronomy 17:19–20, we read of the importance of a daily diet of God's Word for the king. "He must always keep this copy of the law with him and read it daily as long as he lives. That way he will learn to fear the Lord his God by obeying all the terms of this law. *This regular reading will prevent him from becoming proud and acting as if he is above his fellow citizens.* It will also prevent him from turning away from these commands in the smallest way. This will ensure that he and his descendants will reign for many generations in Israel." A regular diet of God's Word is critical to a life of faithful discipleship. If it was a command to the king, those of us who have access to the truth should heed these words as well. Those who have no access, and their leaders, who are often illiterate, walk a perilous road.

Third, discipleship is a call to service. All those who follow Jesus are called to serve. Just as Jesus came not to be served (Luke 22:21-7; John 13:12-17), he called his disciples to a life of service. Paul's single-minded commitment to serving God is seen in 1 Corinthians 7:7-11 where he encouraged others to remain single as he was so they could be more fully devoted to God.

Fourth, discipleship is a call to humility. Philippians 2:4-8 speaks of Christ's voluntary humility. He took upon himself an attitude of untouchability, being below others, to give others dignity and respect. Throughout India, those that have grown up below the caste system have had humility beaten into them, and are forced to look at others as better than themselves. As followers of Jesus, our call is to see others in a similar way, not clinging to our rights, but serving out of love. This applies even within the Christian family (Ephesians 5:22–6:8) where humility brings about self-sacrificing unconditional love, the cornerstone for healthy relationships.

Fifth, discipleship is a call to holiness. Jesus said, "You are my disciples if you keep obeying my teachings" (John 8:31). The Sermon on the Mount is Christ's most specific call to holy living. In it we find how we are to live our lives. There is such great weight assigned to these matters that he closes the sermon with the stern warning that "the

---

50   Scot McKnight, "Jesus Creed," *Christian Century*, 7 September 2004, 23–24.

decisive issue is whether they obey my Father in Heaven" (Matthew 7:21). Those who claim allegiance but do not obey are turned out. Welcomed into the kingdom of heaven are those who obey and endure.

Sixth, discipleship is a call to suffer. Just as Jesus suffered, we too are to expect similar trials as we follow him. Peter said, "This suffering is all part of what God has called you to. Christ, who suffered for you is your example. Follow in his steps" (1 Peter 2:21). The human response to injustice is often retaliation. Scripture directs believers to endure and trust God for the outcome. This is a beautiful picture of the transforming nature of suffering.

In going, the call is to make disciples who obey Jesus. Disciples are called to love God and others, commit themselves to the truth, serve with joy, walk with humility, live holy lives, and face suffering with courage. What he taught is kept for us in his written Word. The ability to read and understand what Jesus said and did is useful to the discipleship process.

Is discipleship possible for the illiterate? They can be, and often are, examples of radical commitment to Jesus. But do disciples benefit from the ability to read the Word of God for themselves? And is it critical that the leaders in the emerging church are able to read the Bible? I believe the answer is an unqualified *yes*.

The Emerging Church
What does the emerging church in India mean? It is important to know what it is and if a literate membership is beneficial. The parameters of this book are limited to the emerging church, which includes congregations that consist of new believers, most of them brand-new congregations themselves. For the most part this does not include churches within mainline denominations, though in some cases these denominational groups are involved in church planting thrusts with new congregation plants in India. The research done for this book was conducted in India alone.

The goal of church planting efforts in India is sustainable, rapidly reproducing congregations. Without this target, the population increase in India will continue to outpace the growth of the church, and hundreds of millions will never have the opportunity to hear of the love of God in Christ Jesus.

Radical Protestant Description
"Your love for one another will prove to the world that you are my disciples"

(John 13:35). The church is a community of disciples who are characterized by love. And nothing attracts the non-believer to Christ like love among the believers. Howard Snyder, in his fine book, *The Radical Wesley,* gives a poignant description of the gathered church of committed believers living in the fellowship of mutual correction, support, and abiding love.[51] He then gives this radical Protestant definition some specifics.

1. Voluntary adult membership based on a covenant commitment to Jesus Christ, emphasizing obedience to Jesus as necessary evidence of faith in him. Believer's baptism has usually been the sign of this commitment, but not always. The point is not fundamentally the *form* of joining the covenant community but the *fact* and *meaning* of conscious committed membership in it.
2. A community or brotherhood of discipline, edification, correction and mutual aid, in conscious separation from the world, as the primary visible expression of the church.
3. A life of good works, service and witness as an expression of Christian love and obedience expected of all believers. Thus, there is an emphasis on the ministry of the laity rather than of a special ministerial class and the church is viewed as "a missionary minority."
4. The Spirit and the Word as comprising the sole basis of authority, implying a de-emphasis on or rejection of church traditions and creeds.
5. Primitivism and restitutionism. The early church is the model, and the goal is to restore the essential elements of early church life and practice. This usually implies some view of the fall of the church as well.
6. A pragmatic, functional approach to church order and structure.
7. A belief in the universal church as the body of Christ, of which the particular visible community is but a part. [52]

This description of the church is not prescriptive, but descriptive. It is simply to point out that the church is comprised of disciples living in loving obedience to Jesus and loving submission to one another. The

---

51   Howard A. Snyder, *The Radical Wesley and Patterns for Church Renewal* (Downers Grove: Inter-Varsity Press, 1980), 113.
52   Ibid., 114.

form and structure will vary. This is not fixed.

The People of the Emerging Church

The emerging church in India is growing at astounding rates outside of existing structures. Many who lead the emerging church movement in North India are committed to the house church model. To them, buildings are anathema. Many, if not most, have Pentecostal leanings. Healings and miracles often lead to and accompany growth. Prayer is almost as regular as breathing. However, it is difficult, if not impossible, to summarize the structure. It is different not just in different places, but also in the same place where God is using several ministries in church planting work. But one feature shares commonality. Most of the new disciples cannot read. Love is present. Community is present. Reliance on the Holy Spirit is a reality. Jesus is worshipped. But without literate leadership at a minimum, this great movement of the Spirit of God could soon collapse or degenerate into a Hindu/Christo paganism. This has the potential to stop the almost miraculous growth of this church.

The sprouting church is arising from the poor, oppressed peoples of Indian society. Rural villages as well as urban slums are the soils from which the emerging church is growing. Many pastors (often illiterate) shepherd ten or more small congregations in neighboring villages. This is not a recipe for sustainable discipleship. With an illiterate membership and significant percentage of illiterate pastors, growth in individual and corporate discipleship is greatly limited. Our concern is that the explosive growth will not result in a church that is a mile wide and an inch deep.

Implications

For the Jew, the written Word was fundamental to their identity just as this is the same for followers of Jesus today. Faith without access to the Bible is unimaginable. Discipleship does not require the ability to read God's truth, but is greatly benefited by it. Loving God and obedience to him is taught through the Scriptures. Church planting strategies among nonliterate communities need to place a high priority on teaching new believers to read.

Chapter 4
The Bible and Reading through the Ages

Andrew Robinson, in his book *The Story of Writing*, begins with the statement, "Writing is among the greatest inventions in human history, perhaps *the* greatest invention, since it made history possible."[53] Today people marvel at the transformation of society brought about by the industrial revolution, the automobile, and, today, the Internet. None of this would have been possible without the written word. For thousands of years, writing has played an important role in human history.

Before serving in my present missions role, I was involved in contract management with a Department of Defense supplier. The relationship between the defense company and the United States government was specified and regulated by a written document, a contract. This spelled out clearly the expectations of both parties. Without this written document to go back to, misunderstandings were bound to occur. This is true for various reasons. Partly because memories are weak and partly because the agreement was complex because of the technical nature of the products produced. It was necessary in part because people tend to be more concerned about protecting their own interests rather than the interests of others. There is conjecture that this was the very reason for the invention of writing 5,000 years ago. "People had earlier realized that verbal instructions, agreements and tallies could be easily garbled, disputed or forgotten. A special witness had been needed, an 'immortal witness,' who could recall aloud amounts and commodities without error, who could be questioned at any time to confirm facts verbally and stop disputes. And so writing was born, at first blush the human voice turned to stone."[54] Andrew Robinson says that "most scholars now accept that writing began with accountancy . . . writing developed

---

53   Andrew Robinson, *The Story of Writing* (London: Thames and Hudson, Ltd., 2003), 7.
54   Steven Rogers Fischer, *A History of Reading* (London: Reaktion Books, 2003), 11.

as a direct consequence of the compelling demands of an expanding economy."[55] In Mesopotamia, "writing developed not to reproduce a pre-existent spoken discourse, but to commit to memory concrete bits of information."[56]

The practical value of writing cannot be underestimated. Christians are known as people of the Book. In God's sovereign plan, He gave us the written Word. Without the written text, it is uncertain where the church would be today. In the next section, there is a brief look at the role of the written text and literacy in Israel before the time of Christ until the advent of the printing press and subsequent Reformation.

Written Tradition in Jewish Life

It is helpful to look back at Jewish history to reflect on the importance of reading. William Barclay tells us about the ceremony carried out on the first day a Jewish boy went to school.

> On the day when he was to go to school for the first time, the boy was wakened early, before dawn, and when it was still dark. He was bathed, and then dressed in a gown "with fringes." As soon as dawn came, he was taken to the Synagogue, by his father, or by a wise friend of the family, if his father was not available. He was put on the reading-desk with a scroll open in front of him at Exodus 20:2–26, the passage which tells of God's revelation of the Law of Moses. That passage was then read aloud as the passage for the day. He was then taken to the house of the teacher, who welcomed him by enfolding him in his arms. He was shown a slate, with the alphabet written on it in various combinations, and with two of the basic texts of the Law—"Moses commanded us a law, even the inheritance of the congregation of Jacob," and, "And the Lord called unto Moses, and spake unto him out of the tabernacle of the congregation." In addition to that there was one further sentence: "The Law will be my calling." These things the teacher read to the lad, and the lad repeated them after the teacher. The slate was then smeared with honey, and the lad was bidden to lick it off. This was in memory of Ezekiel's experience when he ate the scroll: "And it was

55   Robinson, 11.
56   Fischer, 17.

in my mouth as honey for sweetness." Then he was given sweet cakes to eat, with passages from the Law in praise of the Law written on them. Finally there was a prayer to the angels to open the boy's heart and to strengthen his memory and school had begun for another Jewish boy.[57]

This experience would be engrained forever on the heart and mind of the child. The ceremony fed all the senses in an unforgettable manner. If everything went as planned, the child would begin his education tasting the sweetness of the Law and kindling a flame within his bosom to read and understand the book that brings life. For the Jew, education was entirely religious. "There was no textbook except the Scriptures; all primary education was preparation for reading the law; and all higher education was the reading and the study of it."[58] For the Jew, literacy was one of the critical building blocks of a faith structure that provided stability, generational longevity, and depth.

Israelite Literacy

"Jewish piety, as it is seen during the centuries around the beginning of the Christian era, has been appropriately characterized as *torah-centric*. The people of the Covenant knew that they had the incomparable privilege of being entrusted with God's holy Torah, the source of life and salvation; this was accorded an importance which can hardly be exaggerated, and played a central and essential role in the life of the people."[59] The Word of God, transmitted through the written text and memorized, was critical to the life of God's people. "Jewish scribes attributed an immeasurable and inexhaustible wealth of content to the Divine Word. This is particularly true of the Word of Scripture. The task of the people of God, from the scribes' point of view, is by means of the right attitude of listening to, and seeking in the Scriptures, to find out all their divine gifts: their joy and consolation, their warning and punishment, their instruction and teaching, their directives and laws for every situation of life."[60] But, you may ask, did the literacy level have any impact on discipleship of the Israelite people? Gerhardsson's material

---

57   William Barclay, *Educational Ideals in the Ancient World.* (Grand Rapids: Baker, 1977), 12–13.

58   Ibid., 13.

59   Birger Gerhardsson, *Memory and Manuscript: Oral Tradition and Written Transmission in Rabbinic Judaism and Early Christianity* (Grand Rapids: Eerdmans, 1998), 19.

60   Ibid., 33.

supports the premise that the written Word of God was profoundly important to the Jewish community.

Alan Miller, in addressing "The Question of Israelite Literacy," concludes, "Ancient Hebrew written documents, recovered by archaeology, demonstrate both that there were readers and writers in ancient Israel, and that they were by no means rare. Few places would have been without someone who could write, and few Israelites could have been unaware of writing."[61] Morris Watkins says the Israelites "were probably as literate as any people of the ancient world. They were truly a 'people of the Book,' a book that preserved their identity as a nation and as a people of God."[62]

Estimates of Israelite literacy have come under question in recent years. The problem of contemporary data from 2,000 years ago presents unique challenges. It is impossible to observe and question people from ancient cultures, so one of the key research tools is unavailable. In an article entitled "Illiteracy in the Land of Israel in the First Centuries C.E.," the author examined relevant twentieth century data related to the encounter between a traditional and a modern society, that is, Western civilization, which is based on writing. He found that "the more agricultural the society, the higher the percentage of illiterate people."[63] Based on his study of many nations in the nineteenth and twentieth centuries, including the nation of India, he concludes, "There is a close relationship between agriculture and literacy."[64] In addition he says, "There is no reason to confine this social-historical phenomenon to the twentieth or nineteenth centuries. It is most likely that the same worldwide rule was valid in former centuries and in the land of Israel."[65] Another indicator of literacy is infant mortality. In his analysis of contemporary data, he found that "the higher the literacy rate, the lower the number of infant deaths and the higher life expectancy."[66] The data Bar-Ilan gathered supports a literacy rate in Israel somewhere between 3 and 10 percent. "This literacy rate, a small fraction of society,

---

61   Alan R. Millard, "The Question of Israelite Literacy: The Scribes Had No Monopoly on Writing," *Bible Review*, Fall 1987, 31.

62   Morris Watkins, *Literacy, Bible Reading, and Church Growth through the Ages* (Pasadena: William Carey Library, 1978), 5.

63   Meir Bar-Ilan, "Illiteracy in the Land of Israel in the First Centuries C.E.," *Essays in the Social Scientific Study of Judaism and Jewish Society*, II (New York: Ktav, 1992), 50.

64   Ibid., 51.

65   Ibid.

66   Ibid., 54.

though low by modern standards, was not low at all if one takes into account the needs of traditional society in the past."[67]

Ian Young, in his excellent article "Israelite Literacy: Interpreting the Evidence" agrees with Bar-Ilan's research concerning agrarian society and low literacy levels. He says, "Rural patterns of living are inimical to the spread of literacy."[68] Deuteronomy 31:9–13 states:

> So Moses wrote down this law and gave it to the priests, who carried the Ark of the Lord's Covenant, and to the leaders of Israel. Then Moses gave them this command: At the end of every seventh year, the Year of Release, during the Festival of Shelters, you must read this law to all the people of Israel when they assemble before the Lord your God at the place he chooses. Call them together—men, women, children and the foreigners living in your towns—so they may listen and learn to fear the Lord your God and carefully obey all the terms of this law. Do this so that your children who have not known these laws will hear them and will learn to fear the Lord your God. Do this as long as you live in the land you are crossing the Jordan to occupy.

Young states that "the educational ideal . . . is that the priest will read the law before the assembled Israelites. There is no hint that it was considered necessary to educate the people to read it themselves. Thus when the priests failed in their duty, the people suffered from ignorance."[69] It is good to remember the fact that because of limited copies of written texts, it only made sense that a small percentage of the people could access these documents. Availability was a definite factor in the limitations on literacy during the period prior to the invention of the printing press.

There are other passages that seem to indicate that all of Israel was to read. These are Deuteronomy 6:9, 20; 24:1; 27:2–3, 8; Nehemiah 9:3, 38. Young concludes, "These verses need imply nothing more than that a scribe, priest or government official was expected to be within

---

67   Ibid., 58.
68   Ian M. Young, "Israelite Literacy: Interpreting the Evidence Part I," *Vetus Testamentum*, Vol. 48, No. 2, April 1998, 242.
69   Ibid., 243.

reach of every Israelite at need."[70] In Part II of the same article, Young concludes, "The hypothesis that scribes, priests and the upper class formed the literate segment of ancient Israelite society seems to be the best reading of the evidence. Israel was therefore a literate society in that the use of writing was widespread, and was for many a day-to-day part of life. Nevertheless, the majority of the population had access to the literate world only through intermediaries."[71] The leaders were literate and the well-being of Israelite society was dependent on their faithfulness to read God's Word to them so they would know the truth and walk in it. When the leaders were not faithful, perilous times were ahead. In India today, two-thirds of the leaders of the emerging church are unable to read the Holy Scriptures. This does not bode well for discipling the explosive growth of new believers in this idolatrous and syncretistic society.

Literacy in the Life of Jesus

Some argue that Jesus did not write anything we know of. This is supposed to be evidence that literacy is not critical for discipleship. In spite of this, "the teachings of Jesus of Nazareth can be interpreted as moving toward a literate religious culture."[72] Boomershine compares Jesus' teaching methodology with Socrates. He states that both most likely did not write any documents. "The composition of the New Testament writings in the first-second century CE established a tradition that generated the writings of first the Apologists and then the ante-Nicene fathers. . . . Christians established a network of textual communities that produced and distributed a widely diversified literary tradition. Christians were aggressive in the appropriation of the communications technology of literacy."[73] Foundational to the expansion of Christianity, this new communication system was the base "to the expansion of what began as a small Jewish sect into what became, in the fourth century, the dominant religion of the Roman Empire."[74]

---

70   Ibid., 250.

71   Ian M. Young, "Israelite Literacy: Interpreting the Evidence Part II," *Vetus Testamentum*, Vol. 48, No. 3, July 1998, 420.

72   Thomas E. Boomershine, "Jesus of Nazareth and the Watershed of Ancient Orality and Literacy," Semia 65, *Orality and Textuality in Early Christian Literature*, Vol. 65 1995, 29.

73   Ibid., 18.

74   Ibid.

The reasons for rapid expansion of the church are many and varied. Latourette lists several: miracles, purpose in life, moral strength, solid philosophical footing, endorsement by Constantine, disintegration of society, inclusiveness, flexibility and conviction, courage of martyrs, moral transformation and immortality.[75] Morris Watkins reminds us, "As the Gospel spread throughout the Roman world and multitudes were converted in almost every part of the empire, it was impossible for new converts in every place to have an apostle in their midst. They needed someone or something to keep them from going astray – they needed a substitute for an eye witness. Written accounts were the substitute." As Luke told his friend Theophilus, his purpose in writing was "that you may know the truth concerning the things of which you have been informed."[76] The biblical text undergirded the rapid expansion of the Gospel. But the next 1,000 years were a different story. Latourette believes there may have been fewer Christians in AD 1500 than there had been a 1,000 years before.[77]

Reading in the Early Church

During the early centuries of the church, an attempt was made to deny education to Christian children. On December 11 in AD 361, Julian entered Constantinople as the Roman Emperor. "Julian sought to restore paganism...."[78] However, "He deliberately disclaimed any desire to injure Christians."[79] "It was not from any feeling of compassion toward the Christians that he treated them at first with greater humanity than had been evinced by the former persecutors, but because he had discovered that paganism had derived no advantage from their torture, while Christianity had been specially increased, and had become honoured by the fortitude of those who died in defense of the faith."[80] His strategy was much more subtle and insidious. He saw the futility of religious genocide through violence. Instead, "He initiated a mild persecution."[81] His objective was to deprive the church of education.

---

75   Kenneth Scott Latourette, *A History of Christianity Volume I: to A.D. 1500* (New York: Harper and Row, 1975), 105–107.

76   Watkins, 16.

77   Kenneth Scott Latourette, *A History of Christianity Volume II: Reformation to the Present* (New York: Harper and Row, 1975), 2.

78   Latourette, *History of Christianity Volume I: to A.D. 1500*, 160.

79   Barclay, 241.

80   Ibid., 241–242.

81   Ibid., 241.

In a pronouncement the very first year of his reign, "The aim of Julian was quite clear; it was to close the secular schools against all Christian teachers. They must either abandon their belief in Christianity, and return to the belief in the old pagan gods, or cease to teach."[82] Barclay goes on to say that it was clear that his intention was to turn schools into pagan learning centers. The end result would make it impossible for Christian parents to send their children to school. "Julian had reason to expect that in the space of a few years, the church would relapse into its primeval simplicity, and that the theologians, who possessed an inadequate share of the learning and eloquence of the age, would be succeeded by a generation of blind and ignorant fanatics, incapable of defending the truth of their own principles, or of exposing the various follies of polytheism."[83]

Even the pagans themselves were shocked by this act of Julian. Ammianus Marcellinus said of Julian's decree, "But his forbidding masters of rhetoric and grammar to instruct Christians was a cruel action, and was deserving to be buried in everlasting silence."[84] Gregory of Nazianzen says that Julian declared, "Literature and the Greek language are naturally ours, who are worshippers of the gods; illiteracy, ignorance and rusticity are yours, whose wisdom goes no further than to say 'believe.'"[85] Socrates writes, "He enacted a law by which Christians were excluded from the cultivation of literature, lest when they have sharpened their tongue, they should be able the more readily to meet the argument of the heathen. . . . He knew very well that the fables it contains would expose the whole pagan system, of which he had become the champion, to ridicule and contempt."[86]

Fortunately, death came quickly to Julian. Only one year after this decree, he was mortally wounded in battle. His successor rescinded the edict. "The death of Julian saved Christianity from what might well have been a very dangerous situation, for the withholding of all educational rights would have had a most serious effect on the church."[87] Many viewed stripping the church of education as much more dangerous than violence. I wonder what Socrates would say today about the strength

---

82   Ibid., 247.
83   Ibid., 247.
84   Ibid., 248.
85   Ibid., 248.
86   Ibid., 249.
87   Ibid., 250.

and longevity of the emerging church in India, which is unlettered along with most of the leaders as well? I wonder if by ignoring the critical importance of literacy for our new brothers and sisters, we passively adopt Julian's insidious strategy?

Literacy During the Middle Ages

This was a dark period in church history. "These were years of little education and of widespread illiteracy in Europe—years of superstition and corruption in the church. And these were years when Islam overran Southwest Asia, North Africa, and Spain, all but stamping out the Christian church in these lands and blocking the way to the East for 700 years."[88] Two incidences help to capture the setting at the time in relation to literacy.

Heresy is a problem the church has and will face throughout history. Dealing with heresy has often left the church with a tarnished reputation. During the crusades in France in AD 1229, "an ecclesiastical council at Toulouse outlined a stern procedure for the eradication of heresy in the south. Among other measures, the council forbade to the laity the possession of copies of the Bible, except the Psalms and such passages as were in the breviary, and condemned vernacular translations. It thus sought to remove one of the prevalent sources of heresy."[89] It is hard to imagine, but many in the Roman Catholic Church saw the Bible as a dangerous book. This was the time when the Church of Rome substituted fable for faith in Jesus Christ. The written Word of God was unavailable to the people of God. The church slowly yet steadily slipped from protecting biblical truth to protecting its own power interests.

The second incident that captures the essence of the significance of literacy during this time is in the life of John Wycliffe. He challenged the changing and self-serving teachings of the corrupt Church. "In furtherance of his convictions, Wycliffe had the Bible translated from the Vulgate. He insisted that the Scriptures are the supreme authority, that priests and bishops should be familiar with them, and that even unlettered men and simple men can understand them and should read them. To make the Bible accessible to the rank and file, he had it put into the English vernacular of his day."[90] The Word of God read and understood in the language of the people had transforming power. The

---

88   Watkins, 35.
89   Latourette, *History of Christianity Volume I: to A.D. 1500*, 456–57.
90   Latourette, *History of Christianity Volume I: to A.D. 1500*, 664.

church resisted this. And it was not until the advent of the printing press that the impact of this simple principle shook the world.

The Word of God and the Reformation

"It is impossible to overemphasize the importance of the invention of printing by movable type in the mid-fifteenth century."[91] Until this time, ordinary Christians "owned no scriptures or documents and had no access to Scripture except through hearing portions read aloud in church services."[92] It all changed with Gutenberg in Mainz. Through his creative genius and the conditions existing in the fifteenth century, this entrepreneur changed the direction of the world. And change came rapidly. "In 1450 only one printing press was operating in all of Europe. By 1500, around 1,700 presses in over 250 printing centers had already published 27,000 known titles in more than *ten million* copies."[93] According to John Man, the quantity of printed books was "some 15-20 million."[94] In two short generations, the shift from orality to a world of writing launched. "It would be no exaggeration to claim that printing has been as important to humankind as the controlled use of fire and the wheel."[95]

The shift from orality to the written page led to "the unleashing of mechanisms that prompted a new view of self and a spirit of abstraction. . . . It encouraged a logic of the act as well as a logic of the work, and also an ability to reach reasoned decisions and a higher measure of self-control. These were doubtless the printed page's greatest achievements of all."[96] Printing, Luther said, was "God's highest and extremist act of grace, whereby the business of the Gospel is driven forward, freeing Germany from the shackles of Rome."[97] While Luther was studying at the university, he came across a Latin Bible. "Greatly astonished, he observed that it contained far more passages, epistles, and Gospels than were customarily expounded . . . from the pulpits."[98] The printed page

---

91   Watkins, 62.

92   David B. Barrrett, Todd M. Johnson, and Peter F. Crossing, "Missionmetrics 2005: A Global Survey of World Missions," *International Bulletin of Missionary Research*, Vol. 29, No. 1, January 2005, 28.

93   Fischer, 207.

94   John Man, *The Gutenberg Revolution: The Story of a Genius and an Invention that Changed the World* (London: Headline Book Publishing, 2002), 216.

95   Fischer, 213.

96   Ibid., 207.

97   Man, 288.

98   Hans J. Hillerbrand, *The Reformation: A Narrative History Related by Contemporary*

was the fuel of the Reformation and responsible for the development of Western civilization. The alarm bells rung within Catholicism's hierarchy. "At the Fifth Lateran Council in 1515 Pope Leo X prohibited everywhere in Christendom the publishing of any printed work without prior authorization of one of two persons: In Rome, the Vicar of His Holiness or the Master of the Sacred Palace: outside of Rome, the Local bishop or inquisitor."[99] They knew that the Bible in the hands of the people would allow the common person to learn and question. The impenetrable barrier of control maintained by the Catholic Church would be breached. "The emphasis on privilege collapsed as Gutenberg invented moveable type and printed the whole Bible."[100]

"The Book was made accessible to the illiterate and semi-literate masses because it could now be read aloud, heard, remembered and repeated in the vernacular. And the unlettered majority proved to have some ideas of its own. Once the religious basis of legitimation was shifted to The Book in the vernacular, and once the people asserted and believed that no clergy were to have greater interpretive rights than other Christians, the question followed quite naturally as to who had the right to exert the power of influencing others by religious speak, whether by reading, explaining or preaching."[101] Snyder then goes on to say, "The Bible was central to all sixteenth century reform. . . . The reading aloud and hearing of Scripture in the vernacular was a primary agency of reform both inside and outside the Anabaptist movement."[102] Jack Goody says, "The book is clearly an important instrument of power, and it is quite understandable that one sixteenth century poet in England declared the pen to be more powerful than the sword."[103]

People without the ability to read the Word of God for themselves, either because of availability or illiteracy, became convenient pawns of church hierarchy and control. There was no check on absolute power and corruption. Luther himself was able to break free of this bondage because of reading the written Word. He was convinced that all believers needed to read the Bible for themselves. "Protest on the part of the underprivileged classes has often been connected with a movement

---

Observers and Participants (Grand Rapids: Baker, 1978), 23.

99   Fischer, 221.

100 Barrrett, et al., 28.

101 Arnold Snyder, "Orality, Literacy and the Study of Anabaptism," *Mennonite Quarterly Review*, Vol. 55, No. 4, October 1991, 381.

102 Ibid., 390.

103 Goody, 155.

toward universal literacy. . . ."[104] In an article on literacy and domination, M. G. Brett highlights the text from Deuteronomy 31: 24–29.

> When Moses had finished writing down this entire body of law in a book, he gave these instructions to the Levites who carried the Ark of the Lord's Covenant: "Take this Book of the Law and place it beside the Ark of the Covenant of the Lord your God, so it may serve as a witness against the people of Israel. For I know how rebellious and stubborn you are. Even now, while I am still with you, you have rebelled against the Lord. How much more rebellious will you be after my death! Now summon all the leaders and officials of your tribes so that I can speak to them and call heaven and earth to witness against them. I know that after my death you will become utterly corrupt and will turn from the path I have commanded you to follow. In the days to come, disaster will come down on you, for you will make the Lord very angry by doing what is evil in his sight."

"This passage suggests that the Book of the Law was to function as a 'witness' against all those who were in authority, including the Levites, since these authorities were sure to become corrupt."[105] Without the writing down of the Law, this critical check on leadership would not exist. "Writing has been endowed with the potential function of critique. Critique is made possible by the 'external' and public measure of the Law being written down."[106]

Jacques Ellul makes a fascinating observation on the same subject of power and domination. "The cathedrals were erected to the glory of God, certainly; but they attested the indisputable power of the church. These images are associated with the determination of the princes of the church to dominate society."[107] He is convinced that the written Word is critical. "The Word is the place to begin. . . . We must restore its royal domain and its demands. The enormous mutation made possible by biblical revelation assures us that this effort does not amount to a

---

104   Ibid., 164.
105   M. G. Brett, "Literacy and Domination: G. A. Herion's Sociology of History Writing," *Journal of the Study of the Old Testament*, Issue 37, February 1987, 29.
106   Ibid., 29.
107   Jacques Ellul, *The Humiliation of the Word* (Grand Rapids: Eerdmans, 1985), 185.

pointless venture or an attempt to try out a risky path."[108]

Sola Scriptura

Biblical faith is based upon the written Word. This statement does not dismiss the importance of general revelation, but only correctly elevates the importance of the revealed will of God made known through the Scriptures. The written Word was not just intended for the educated elite. "*Sola Scriptura*"—by Scripture *alone*—is a reformation slogan that stands for the reformer's total view of how the Bible should function as an authority in the conscience of the individual and in the church's corporate life."[109] Martin Luther was the pioneer. "Many have traced how . . . that to hear or read the Scripture is nothing else than to hear God . . . Luther was led to set the authority of 'the infallible Word of God' over that of popes, councils, church fathers, and tradition in all its forms."[110] It is the written Word that penetrated the mind and heart of Luther through the work of the Holy Spirit. This set off an explosion that changed the course of human history. Without the introduction of the printing press and the ability to read, the Bible would have remained a closed book to most people and provided little fuel to encourage and sustain the Reformation.

Paul's instructions to Timothy form the pivotal passage for the importance of the written Word in discipling the believer. "All Scripture is inspired by God and is useful to teach us what is true and to make us realize what is wrong in our lives. It straightens us out and teaches us to do what is right. It is God's way of preparing us in every way, fully equipped for every good thing God wants us to do" (2 Timothy 3:16–17).

There are several points that need to be made concerning this passage as it relates to literacy in the emerging church in India. First, Paul tells Timothy "All Scripture" is useful in preparing followers of Jesus Christ. For a leader, such as Timothy, to use the written text, it is safe to assume he had access to and the ability to read. Expecting leaders of the new churches in India to fully equip the people under their care without the ability to read the Word of God for themselves is shortsighted. And if the goal is rapidly reproducing church planting movements, one of the important objectives should be to bring literacy

---

108   Ibid., 254.
109   John Warwick Montgomery, editor, *God's Inerrant Word: An International Symposium on the Trustworthiness of Scripture* (Minneapolis: Bethany, 1974), 43.
110   Ibid., 43.

to the emerging church so it can expand even more explosively.

Second, Paul's choice of the word *useful* (or "profitable") is intriguing. "Now by virtue of the fact that 'all scripture' is God-breathed, it is *useful* or *beneficial* or *profitable*. It is a very practical, yes, an indispensable, instrument or tool *for the teacher*" (implied here).[111] I do not believe Paul's choice of the word is to indicate a decreased importance of the Scripture in the discipling of the believer. The Word of God is useful or profitable "because it is inspired by God."[112]

Then Paul goes on to tell Timothy what the Scriptures are useful for. He lists four items that result in a fully equipped disciple of Jesus. (1) "Teaches us what is true"—this is a positive instruction to impart in the followers of Jesus, the truth found in the pages of the Scriptures. (2) "Makes us realize what is wrong in our lives"—warnings based on the Word of God must be given. Errors in doctrine and life must be "patiently corrected" (2 Timothy 4:2). (3) "It straightens us out"— those who are on the wrong path must be convinced of their error and redirected in their pursuit of holiness. (4) "Teaches us to do what is right"—the teacher must train his people to live disciplined lives reflecting the good God wants us to do.

The Christian faith is a faith with a book. Without knowing the Scriptures, the life of the believer will more often be likened to the seed planted in the rocky soil. It quickly sprang up, but with a weak root system, it could not survive the normal stresses of life. The ability to read and understand God's Word is a great benefit to a growing and maturing faith. Without literacy, followers of Jesus Christ will not only be limited in their ability to know the true and living God, they are more likely to succumb to temptation and heresy and remain trapped in the bondages common for all of us.

Is it important that the new churches in India have access to the Scriptures? Is it enough that they have Bible stories handed down orally?

God revealed himself to us not only through the person of Jesus Christ, but through the written page. When tempted, our Savior used the phrase, "It is written" three times to defeat the attack of the devil. "The use of this term in the NT was an inheritance, not an invention. The idea of a 'canon' or 'Sacred Scriptures' was handed down to Christianity

---

111 William Hendriksen, *New Testament Commentary, Exposition of the Pastoral Epistles* (Grand Rapids: Baker, 1978), 303.

112 John R. W. Stott, *The Message of 2 Timothy: Guard the Gospel* (Downers Grove: Inter-Varsity Press, 1973), 102.

from Judaism. . . . Whatever stood written in these Scriptures was a word of God, and was therefore referred to indifferently as something which 'Scripture says.'"[113] God chose to preserve and protect his will and purpose with the written Word, to reveal himself through the written page and face temptation quoting the very same Scriptures. It is beyond the scope of this book to define or build the case for what Scripture is. I am working under the assumption that the readers accept the Bible (the 66 books of the Old and New Testaments) is the revealed will of God and necessary in the discipling process. However, the question remains: Does the ability to *read* the Word of God play an important role in the discipling process?

The emerging church in India is rapidly expanding. Given humanity's sinful nature, issues of power and corruption will go unchecked. Already India excels in these two matters. The written Word must be readable by leaders and believers. It is unwise not to learn from history. The life and growth of discipleship will be short without literate disciples.

Implications

Reading has been an important part of Jewish and Christian religious life. If this is the case historically, it is reasonable to assume that it is no different today. Luther was a leader in setting the authority of the Scriptures over that of the Pope and tradition. Today one must maintain the authority of the Scriptures over church leaders that may or may not respect truth or be able to engage with the truth because of reading blindness. In India, where syncretism is encouraged by a religion that can easily absorb almost any belief system, access to truth remains as vital today as it was thousands of years ago.

---

113   Benjamin Breckinridge Warfield, *The Inspiration and Authority of the Bible* (Philadelphia: Presbyterian and Reformed, 1970), 229.

Chapter 5
Orality and Literacy

The train of orality is picking up steam in missions circles today. The Lausanne Committee for World Evangelism viewed it as important enough to deserve a forum at the Lausanne Conference in September of 2004 in Thailand. The basic premise is that most of the unreached peoples are oral learners and not adequately engaged by the written page or a literate approach to thinking and teaching. In order for the Great Commission to be accomplished, we must change our approach from methods rooted in literate thinking to storytelling. But does this train, which is picking up more and more willing passengers as its speed increases, need some course corrections? Several presuppositions appear weak and have the potential of actually slowing down discipling efforts.

Literacy and Orality

Literacy and orality movements are partners, not antagonists. The acceptance of one does not negate the value of the other. Methodologies promoted by the Orality Movement are useful in the discipling process whether or not the person is literate. It will play an important role in the completion of the Great Commission.

According to the Lausanne Occasional Paper No. 54 coming out of the issue group on orality at the 2004 forum for World Evangelism, the value of both orality and literacy is clear. "Experience shows that once oral learners accept the Gospel, some will have the desire and persistence to become literate in order to read the Bible for themselves. The development of oral strategies is not a deterrent to translating the Bible into every language. In fact, the opposite is true. These burgeoning church planting movements that result from an oral proclamation will need the whole counsel of God."[114] The group does not deny or minimize the importance of the written Word. They then go on to say,

---

114 Lausanne Occasional Paper No. 54, "Making Disciples of Oral Learners," *Lausanne Committee for World Evangelization*, Pattaya, Thailand, 2004, 12.

"We do not want our call for oral approaches to be seen as setting oral and literate approaches in opposition to one another. It is not a matter of 'either-or,' but 'both-and.'"[115]

It is important for the purpose of this book to look critically at the arguments for lifting up the oral tradition. Much of the unevangelized world is nonliterate. This is certainly true of India. On the website of Chronological Bible Storying, they state, "At least 1.5 billion people in the world have never been introduced to reading and writing," and "at least 67 percent of the world's people are either non-literate or functionally illiterate."[116]

One of the impressions gathered from this information is that reading is unnatural. If much of the world remains illiterate, then perhaps this is evidence that orality is the natural way humans communicate as designed by the Creator. Literacy, though useful, is unnatural and perhaps even unneeded in the discipling process. Frank Smith proposes in his fascinating book on reading, *Unspeakable Acts, Unnatural Practices,* that "learning and comprehension are simply states of the human organism"[117] and that "reading is the most natural activity in the world."[118] He goes on to explain:

> I am not taking liberties with language here. The word *reading* is properly employed for all manner of activities when we endeavor to make sense of circumstances; its original meaning was "interpretation." We read the weather, the state of the tides, people's feelings and intentions, stock market trends, animal tracks, maps, signals, signs, symbols, palms, tea leaves, the law, music, mathematics, minds, body language, between the lines, and above all. . . we read faces. . . Researcher Daniel McNeill (1998) explains how 22 pairs of facial muscles are constantly orchestrated to display at least 4,000 different expressions, all produced and understood without any instruction at all. Some basic expressions of emotion—such as fear, anger, surprise, disgust, sadness, and enjoyment—may be instinctive, but the majority are learned

---

115   Ibid., 13.
116   *Fast Facts: On Orality, Literacy and Chronological Bible Storying,* http://www.chrono-logicalbiblestorying.com/articles/fast_facts.htm.
117   Ibid., 5.
118   Ibid., 9.

early in life. These expressions, involving the entire face from the corners of the mouth to the eyebrows, each element operating individually, communicate not just physical states, but agreement, disagreement, encouragement, puzzlement, disbelief, collusion, threat, challenge—and of course interest and desire. When was anyone taught to interpret all this, to read faces?[119]

Smith, a language researcher and educator, concludes that "reading print is as natural as reading faces. Learning to read should be as natural as any other comprehensible aspect of existence."[120]

Even though Frank Smith has written this book as an educator without acknowledging the Creator, his proposition could be stated in biblical terminology, as reading is part of being an image-bearer of the divine. "Learning and comprehension are simply states of the human organism. They are neither skills nor processes, but a condition of being alive. Their presence in human beings does not have to be explained, only their absence, or rather the consequences of their suppression."[121]

The world's poor and oppressed have been suppressed in reading, often a direct result of exploitation. This was illustrated in chapter 1 as seen in the life of Fredrick Douglass. Reading was a direct threat to the powerful. Making disciples is a transformative process that includes the spiritual without excluding the person as a whole. Illiteracy is at the root of poverty and is often the foundation for exploitation, oppression, and injustice. The Orality Movement, in its God-given zeal to reach the unreached, also needs to include in its emphasis the importance of literacy and its link with humans as image bearers of the divine.

On the other side of the fence is Werner Kelber. He sees the oral tradition as preeminent and the transition of the oral to the written form reducing its power and authority. "The Gospel—like most texts from antiquity—was meant to be read aloud and heard."[122] Most people will agree with Kelber if the statement is taken alone. However, he then goes on to criticize the value of text over the oral tradition. "Literacy

---

119 Ibid., 9–11.
120 Ibid., 13.
121 Ibid., 5.
122 Werner H. Kelber, *The Oral and Written Gospel: The Hermeneutics of Speaking and Writing in the Synoptic Tradition, Mark, Paul and Q* (Philadelphia: Fortress Press, 1983), 217.

is so implanted in every twentieth-century biblical scholar that it is difficult to avoid thinking of it as the normal means of communication and the sole measure of language."[123] He then praises the oral tradition: "Variability and stability, conservatism and creativity, evanescence and unpredictability all mark the pattern of oral tradition."[124] According to Kelber, Paul's assertion, "'Do not go beyond what is written,' is a wholly exceptional statement in Pauline theology, and in making it the apostle has at this point sanctioned the written medium as the basis of the new wisdom. Paul . . . is a subtle but consistent promoter of the values of literacy. In this one case at least we must say that Paul, the oral traditionalist, has activated the powers of the written medium for the purpose of rupturing the oral synthesis."[125] The preeminence Kelber assigns to the oral tradition reduces the authority of the written word. This is wholly logical given the continual changes that occur in human memory. Of course, there also exist textual changes in written documents because of scribal errors, but without a written text, there is nothing to measure change against.

People need to hear the Bible in our churches, not just silently read. This is the pattern in most churches today. The Word of God is read and then explained by the teacher/pastor. People do not gather for worship to simply sit in a pew and read the Bible silently. In many ways the current pattern existing in evangelical congregations caters to people who may not necessarily read. Preaching can be and often is orality in practice. Effective communicators, like the Lord Jesus, tell stories to communicate truth. But oral tradition must be grounded in the enduring written Word to remain consistent with the truth.

Some argue that the Scripture was preserved for generations, perhaps millenniums, orally. James Slack says, "From the time of the creation and the fall until the time of Moses, God did not find it necessary to inspire anyone to record in written form what throughout this period had been God's words and deeds that had been revealed and perpetuated orally. For a few thousand years from Adam and Eve to Abraham, to Joseph and to Moses, the revealed Word of God existed only in oral form."[126] Slack again uses this same argument for the oral

---

123   Ibid., 332.

124   Ibid., 333.

125   Ibid., 177.

126   James B. Slack, "Oral Memory and Its Implications Concerning Chronological Bible Storying," (September 2004, 3rd ed.), 6. http://www.newwway.org/articles/OralMem-

tradition preceding the New Testament documents: "God did not inspire any of His followers to put His revealed Word that came through Christ's teachings and events into written form. God was pleased for His spoken word to remain oral and not written during the period when the Gospel spread throughout the known world and 'turned that world upside down.'"[127] One could reason then of the enduring and verbatim nature of oral memory, at least among the Israelites. However, the issue is not just a matter of memory but of inspiration. All Scripture is "God breathed" (see 2 Timothy 3:16). Neither its accuracy nor its authority is based upon human memory. God was in control of the process and without his direct involvement, the written text we have today would be perilously flawed.

Today, we see the American culture attracted to orality in its preoccupation with film: at the theater, through DVDs, and on television. The powerful magnetism of the story mesmerizes a nation. And it is not just here. In India today, they produce more films than anywhere else in the world. When a book is produced as a film, those who enjoyed reading the text, anxiously await its release. Dominique Lapierre's book, *City of Joy*, is an excellent account of the commitment and transformational impact a Catholic priest had on a slum in Calcutta. The film depicted the almost unbearable living conditions in the slums, but did not include any impact made by this sacrificial committed priest. It apparently was not important to either the screenplay writer (the storyteller) or perhaps the producer to include this positive theme from the book. The written text was modified to better fit the needs of the storyteller. It is true that unless someone had actually read the text, they would be unaware of the change in the storyline. For them, the actual content of the story is what they witnessed on the movie screen. Stories retold without the baseline and authority of a fixed text, continually change and adapt, even in written form. Stories communicated orally, especially from an illiterate leadership in the emerging church in India to an illiterate membership, will follow the same pattern with even fewer boundaries.

One of the problems the Orality Movement must address is the adaptation that occurs when stories are retold. Again, in the Lausanne document, we read, "Providing an 'oral Bible' allows God's Word to

---

oryandImplication.pdf
127   Ibid., 8.

be produced accurately from memory for the purpose of retelling."[128] There is little evidence to support this. Stories change from one person to another. Not only do stories change in this manner, but also human memories are weak, and, as Kelber says above, "Variability and stability, conservatism and creativity, evanescence and unpredictability all mark the pattern of oral tradition."[129] This is not indicative of accuracy in retelling biblical stories from memory. The problem in India today is not that the Bible is unavailable to most people so that orality is the only alternative. The Bible is available to 96 percent of the population. According to the 1991 census data, 96.3 percent of all Indians speak scheduled languages that are all written.[130] For just under 4 percent, oral transmission is the only alternative at this time in history. But where language is written, literacy has been denied to the poor, oppressed communities so they will remain subservient. An oral Bible is good, and in some places necessary. But bringing literacy to the emerging church, especially to the leadership, should also be a clear objective of mission efforts. Without it, distortion of biblical truth is inevitable.

Some argue that literacy is good but not necessarily beneficial for discipleship. This is because of the belief that the memory of the illiterate is much stronger than those that are lettered and therefore they can carry the Bible with them in their mind. Plato decided that writing would ruin the memory and that oral man remembered much better than his literate counterparts.[131] Many tell tales of phenomenal feats of memory in such cultures. Is it really critical that reading the Word of God is necessary for a strong and healthy church?

Jack Goody, a British anthropologist during much of the last century, investigated Plato's well-accepted theory. He worked among the LoDagaa people of northern Ghana. In 1950 he decided to record a sacred ceremony called the Bagre that was part of the initiation rites of an association that provided medical and other benefits. The village reciter, Bemina, convinced him that it was a fixed recitation that people knew by heart and that was handed down in more or less an exact form. This went from generation to generation. Jack sat with Bemina for 10 days recording word for word the Bagre ceremony. Twenty years later, in 1970, he returned to the village now to make recordings of the Bagre

---

128   Lausanne Occasional Paper No. 54, 6.
129   Kelber, 333.
130   *Central Institute of Indian Languages*, http://www.ciil.org/languages/indian.html.
131   Goody, 27.

ceremony. Portable tape recorders were now available and this made his work much easier. Over the next several years he recorded 15 versions. The differences were large. They were significant even when the same man recited on different occasions and greater still when different men recited on the same occasion (for the myth had to be recited three times on each occasion.) Between nearby settlements, the differences were enormous. For example, the number of lines recited varied from 24 to 6133.[132] Jack Goody gave up the notion that the Bagre was fixed. Since there was no fixed text to correct errors, variation was constantly creeping in, partly due to forgetting, partly due to unconscious attempts at improvement, adjustment, creation. He determined that "oral memory is, of course, simply experience reworked."[133] He states, "In oral societies each performance of a long poem, such as the Bagre, reshapes the work and (since performance is transmission) provides a new model for future versions. The process of composition, in the sense of the original act of creation, is impossible to reconstruct for lack of evidence or lack of relevance."[134] As a result of this constant changing inherent in an oral culture, "there can be no true orthodoxy without a 'fixed text' of some kind or other, often arbitrary."[135]

The critical problem faced in an oral culture is preserving the text in the minds of the hearers. Is this probable without some sort of literate, textual transmission? Goody again comments: "Religions in oral cultures are not boundary-maintaining in the same way as those of written cultures. African religions, for example, are generally eclectic [much like Hinduism] without any precise boundaries, a sum of what everybody believes rather than something fixed in a text. As a result, there are constant additions to the corpus of religious activities, some cults disappearing and new ones emerging. With ritual and similar cultural activities, practices change quite rapidly."[136] His conclusion is staggering: "In the domains of ritual and religion, oral cultures are constantly changing."[137] This is consistent with Kelber's statement above. Verbatim memory only becomes possible and valued with literacy.

---

132 Ibid., 36–37.
133 Ibid., 40.
134 Ibid., 44.
135 Ibid., 45.
136 Ibid., 121.
137 Ibid., 124.

John Harvey, in an article on "Orality and Its Implications for Biblical Studies: Recapturing an Ancient Paradigm," also agrees with Goody's conclusions. According to Harvey, "It is also true that a largely oral culture promotes the development of memory skills. Those memory skills, however, tend to emphasize thematic rather than verbatim recall."[138] "In assessing more realistically the nature of verbal memory in primary oral cultures, the work of Milman Parry and Albert Lord again proved revolutionary.... Parry's work with Homeric poems focused the issue. Parry demonstrated that the Iliad and the Odyssey were basically oral creations, whatever circumstances governed their commitment to writing. At first blush, this discovery would seem to have confirmed the assumption of verbatim memorization."[139]

> Parry's work showed that metrically tailored formulas controlled the composition of the ancient Greek epic and that the formulas could be shifted around quite handily without interfering with the storyline or the tone of the epic. Did oral singers actually shift the formulas, so that the individual metrically regular renditions of the same story differed in wording? Or was the story mastered verbatim, so that it was rendered the same way at every performance? Since pre-textual Homeric poets had all been dead for well over 2,000 years, they could not be taped for direct evidence. But direct evidence was available from living narrative poets in modern Yugoslavia, a country adjacent to and in part overlapping ancient Greece. Parry found such poets composing oral epic narrative, for which there was no text. Their narrative poems, like Homer's, were metric and formulaic, although their verse meter happened to be a different one from the ancient Greek dactylic hexameter. Lord continued and extended Parry's work, building up the massive collection of oral recordings of present-day Yugoslav narrative poets now in the Parry Collection at Harvard University.

> Most of these living South Slavic narrative poets—and indeed all of the better ones—are illiterate. Learning to read and

---

138   John D. Harvey, "Orality and Its Implications for Biblical Studies: Recapturing an Ancient Paradigm," *Journal of the Evangelical Theological Society*, 45 (1), 102.

139   Walter J. Ong, *Orality and Literacy: The Technologizing of the Word* (London: Methuen & Co., 1982), 58.

write disables the oral poet, Lord found: it introduces into his mind the concept of a text as controlling the narrative and thereby interferes with the oral composing processes, which have nothing to do with texts but are "the remembrances of songs sung."[140]

This is a far different conclusion than the one purported by the Orality Movement that learning to read greatly reduces one's memory capacity. Memory in an oral culture is not verbatim. Literacy opens the door for people to think in this category. This is also consistent with Jack Goody's findings.

Jim Slack has done a good deal of work on orality and Chronological Bible Storying. He has brought a great deal to light on these subjects. However, the conclusions he has come to on the memory of illiterates are not supported by research. He states of the illiterate, "They have the ability to tell that story immediately, just as it was told to them. Literates lose those memory skills as they change their mind from that of an oral communicator to a literate communicator. A literate has trouble telling a story accurately. That is not the case with oral communicators."[141] Unfortunately, research does not support this thesis. Walter Ong's work sheds more light on this faulty presupposition.

Oral poets' memory of songs is agile: it was "not unusual" to find a Yugoslav bard singing "from ten to twenty syllable lines a minute" (Lord 1960, p. 17). Comparison of the recorded songs, however, reveals that, though metrically regular, they were never sung the same way twice. Basically the same formulas and themes recurred, but they were stitched together or "rhapsodized" differently in each rendition even by the same poet, depending on audience reaction, the mood of the poet or of the occasion, and other social and psychological factors.
The memory feats of these oral bards are remarkable, but they are unlike those associated with memorization of texts. Literates are usually surprised to learn that the bard planning to retell the story he has heard only once wants often to wait a

---

140   Ibid., 59.
141   James Slack, "What Specifically is Chronological Bible Storying?" *Exploring the Implications of Orality, Literacy and Chronological Storying Concerning Global Evangelism,* 2001 *Adjunct* 8, 2.

day or so after he had heard the story before he himself repeats it. In memorizing a written text, postponing its recitation generally weakens recall. An oral poet is not working with texts or in a textual framework. He needs time to let the story sink into his own store of themes and formulas, time to 'get with' the story. In recalling and retelling the story, he has not in any literate sense 'memorized' its metrical rendition from the version of the other singer—a version long gone forever when the new singer is mulling over the story for his own rendition. The fixed materials in the bard's memory are a float of themes and formulas out of which all stories are variously built.[142]

Again it is important to interject that oral memory is not fixed. One of the most telling discoveries in the Lord's work is that, although singers are aware that two different singers never sing the same song exactly alike, nevertheless a singer will protest that he can do his own version of a song line-for-line and word-for-word any time, and indeed, 'just the same twenty years from now.' When, however, their purported verbatim renditions are recorded and compared, they turn out to be never the same, though the songs are recognizable versions of the same story.[143]

It is presumptive and unsubstantiated to believe that an "oral Bible" allows God's Word to be produced "accurately from memory." As can be seen from the above illustrations, verbatim recall is not part of an oral society's thought process. If there is no perception of text, there is nothing to "accurately" recall. Israel's history reminds us of this. In 2 Chronicles 34:14, the high priest "found the Book of the Law of the Lord as it had been given through Moses." When it was read to King Josiah, "he tore his clothes in despair." It is also important to remember that Josiah was a king whose desire it was to obey the Lord. He was not rebelling against the Lord's commands. Yet, even with his reforms, memory of God's Word was limited. Without the written Word regularly read, Israel quickly fell away. Of course, there are other reasons contributing to this precipice moment. But it was the written Word read that awakened the people of God and drew them back from near disaster.

---

142   Ibid., 59–60.
143   Ibid., 61

If accurate memory is more of a dream than a reality, how is it possible to avoid syncretism without the ability to read the Word of God? Syncretism is "the mixing of Christian assumptions with those worldview assumptions that are incompatible with Christianity so that the result is not biblical Christianity."[144] For example, in India syncretism exists when people "consider Jesus just another of many human manifestations of one of their deities."[145] "Syncretism weakens the church, warps non-Christians' understanding of Christianity and withholds from God the full devotion and complete obedience that is rightly due to Him. So the spiritual health and vibrancy of Christian churches depends on developing a faith that is as free from syncretism as possible, a faith that is both biblical and culturally relevant."[146]

The "Making Disciples of Oral Learners" Issue Group at Lausanne proposed four strategies to avoid syncretism among oral learners. "The first key element in avoiding syncretism is communication with people in their mother tongue—the language in which they learned their religion, values, and cultural identity."[147] Most languages do not have the Bible available in print and many languages are purely oral.

> Indeed, language is so overwhelmingly oral that of all the many thousands of languages—possibly tens of thousands—spoken in the course of human history, only around 106 have been ever committed to writing to a degree sufficient to have produced literature, and most have never been written at all. There is as yet no way to calculate how many languages have disappeared or been transmuted into other languages before writing came along. Even now hundreds of languages in active use are never written at all: no one has worked out an effective way to write them. The basic orality of language is permanent.[148]

Given this information, oral communication remains a critical part of communicating the love of Christ to those unable to read for

---

144 Charles Kraft, "Culture, Worldview and Contextualization," *Perspectives on the World Christian Movement*, 3rd ed. Ed. Ralph D. Winter and Stephen Hawthorne (Pasadena: William Carey Library, 1999), 390.

145 Ibid.

146 Lausanne Occasional Paper No. 54, 23.

147 Ibid., 23.

148 Ong, 7.

whatever reason. And it is logical that this makes the most impact in the mother tongue. In India today, most of the evangelism taking place is mother tongue evangelism. Indigenous grass-roots workers do this in their own language among their own people. Most of these people also speak several languages with the majority also able to communicate in their state language. In fact, the church is growing so rapidly among illiterate communities that two-thirds of local churches have illiterate leaders. But at least this is in the heart language of the people.

The second key element in reducing syncretism is to develop discipling resources that are worldview specific. "Generic discipleship materials are insufficient."[149] The point the authors are making here is that the "best discipling resource among oral learners is not a printed booklet but the obedient Christian."[150] The best discipling resource for any learner, be they well educated or not, is an obedient Christian. Christianity is a community of love in which relationships are the key to discipleship. The apostle Paul says in Philippians 4:9, "Keep putting into practice all you learned from me and heard from me and saw me doing, and the God of peace will be with you."

"The third key element in discipling oral learners in order to limit syncretism is to recognize the importance of stories in transforming a person's worldview."[151] N. T. Wright says, "Stories thus provide a vital framework for experiencing the world. They also provide a means by which views of the world may be challenged."[152] Further he says, "Stories are, actually, peculiarly good at modifying or subverting other stories and their worldviews. Where head-on attack would certainly fail, the parable hides the wisdom of the serpent behind the innocence of the dove, gaining entrance and favour which can then be used to change assumptions which the hearer would otherwise keep hidden away for safety. . . . Stories, in having this effect, function as complex metaphors."[153]

Jesus used stories in his teaching. "Jesus' stories are no mere illustrations but 'weapons of warfare.' They draw people into a seemingly innocuous story only to confront them with the demands of discipleship

---

149   Lausanne Occasional Paper No. 54, 24.
150   Ibid.
151   Ibid.
152   N. T. Wright, *The New Testament and the People of God* (Minneapolis: Fortress Press, 1992), 39.
153   Ibid., 40.

in ways that subvert conventional religious tradition and expectation."[154] Wright also makes the following comment about Jesus' teaching.

> Telling stories was (according to the synoptic Gospels) one of Jesus' most characteristic modes of teaching. And, in the light of the entire argument so far, it would be clearly quite wrong to see these stories as mere illustrations of truths that could in principle have been articulated in a purer, more abstract form. They were ways of breaking open the worldview of Jesus' hearers, so that it could be remolded into the worldview which he, Jesus, was commending. His stories, like all stories in principle, invited his hearers into a new world, making the implicit suggestion that the new worldview be tried on for size with a view to permanent purchase.[155]

A question to the Issue Group at Lausanne is, are not stories just as useful in transforming a literate's worldview? Today, the most effective teachers and preachers use stories to break down barriers and penetrate the heart of the individual. Wright again comments, "Stories, never unpopular with children and those who read purely for pleasure, have thus become fashionable of late also among scholars, not least in the biblical studies guild."[156]

"The fourth key element in order to avoid syncretism is to provide a recorded 'oral Bible' for each people group in their language. This is a recorded set of stories, biblically accurate and told in the worldview context."[157] Oral Bibles can be useful in the discipling process of illiterate believers. It certainly provides a baseline that will reduce "evanescence and variability," as Kelber relates above.

Of the four points made by the Orality Issue Group at Lausanne in 2004 in avoiding syncretism among oral learners, the first three apply to all peoples. All missionaries and pastors need to learn mother tongue communication, obedient Christian modeling, and use stories to transform one's worldview. These are effective tools in the hands of persons committed to fulfilling the Great Commission. The church's

---

154 Craig L. Bloomberg, *Jesus and the Gospels: An Introduction and Survey* (Nashville: Broadman & Holman Publishers, 1997), 258.

155 Wright, 77.

156 Ibid., 39.

157 Lausanne Occasional Paper No. 54, 26.

effectiveness in completing this task will significantly increase using these strategies. The fourth strategy, using oral Bibles, can be effective with nonliterates. Oral Bibles are a compilation of stories from the Word of God. Certainly they do not contain the whole counsel of God. The long-term objective would be to provide these people with the written Word and the ability to actually read it.

In India today, the Bible is translated into all the major languages. And yet in rural areas, well over 50 percent of the people are illiterate (at least according to government data). The survey that follows in chapter 8 reveals the low literacy rate among new believers in India today (approximately 10 percent). What is more alarming though is that two-thirds of the leaders are illiterate. Syncretism is almost inevitable. And the expanding church is multiplying in homes. We have new leaders teaching and leading new believers without the ability to read the Word of God for themselves. Certainly Bible stories will be a blessing to the people. But these leaders need to learn to read. The precipice Josiah was at during his reign will quickly swallow the rapidly expanding, but biblically blind, emerging church. The immediate challenge that must not be ignored and aggressively pursued is to set a clear target of literate leadership in the emerging church in India. This is a core need in India today.

The Issue Group at Lausanne had an important role in elevating the use of oral techniques to reach those outside the traditional literate methods of evangelism. Perhaps the church will hear this important message and begin teaching oral strategies in Bible colleges and seminaries. Some missionaries will hear and awaken to this call. In all of this, it is good to remember Walter Ong's advice, "Orality is not the ideal, and never was. To approach it positively is not to advocate it as a permanent state for any culture. Literacy opens possibilities to the word and to human existence unimaginable without writing. Oral cultures today value their oral traditions and agonize over the loss of these traditions, but I have never encountered or heard of an oral culture that does not want to achieve literacy as soon as possible."[158]

Implications

Orality is a positive strategy for discipleship. The major teaching methodologies of orality will benefit the church in general, provide useful tools for Western cross-cultural missionaries, and add value in the evangelism and discipleship process especially where literacy is absent.

---

158   Ong, 175.

However, an important part of this methodology is based on a flawed assumption. Research does not support the premise that illiterates can accurately recall what they have heard. Verbatim memory is only possible with literacy. Oral disciples and even oral leaders are limited in their ability to retain the basic biblical foundations for enduring discipleship. New disciples need to open their eyes to read God's Word. In India today, the emerging church is growing rapidly. An important task of the disciple-maker is to see that the Word of God is available to, at a minimum, the leadership of these churches. Not all disciples need to be able to read the Bible for themselves. But they must regularly hear the Word from their leadership.

Chapter 6
Literacy and Loving Our Neighbor

Loving our neighbor includes responding to the injustices that confine him to life under oppression. Is it enough to preach Christ to a bonded slave and feel our job is done when he responds positively to Christ's love? In this chapter we will examine our role in holistic transformation of those responding to the Gospel in India today, mostly coming from the poor, casteless, and tribal areas. Galatians 6:10 says, "Whenever we have the opportunity, we should do good to everyone, especially to our Christian brothers and sisters." Do followers of Jesus have any responsibility to the nonliterate, especially to those who are brothers and sisters in Christ? The Bible is clear. In Isaiah 58:6, God tells Isaiah to speak these words to the people of Israel: "No, the kind of fasting I want calls you to free those who are wrongly imprisoned and to stop oppressing those who work for you. Treat them fairly and give them what they earn." Solomon says in Proverbs 24:11, "Rescue those who are unjustly sentenced to death; don't stand back and let them die. Don't try to avoid responsibility by saying you didn't know about it."

The Two Great Commandments
Over the past 100 years the evangelical community has focused on the proclamation of the Gospel (the Great Commission) in its mission efforts. Many view the efforts to bring about social change with suspicion. But this has not always been so. I am astounded at Jesus' statement to the religious leader who asked what he had to do to inherit eternal life. Jesus said, "Sell all you have and give the money to the poor, and you will have treasure in heaven. Then come, follow me" (Luke 18:22). There are many ways to view this teaching. Clearly, one of the lessons Jesus taught was that possessions are not for personal consumption alone, but for sharing with the needy. He, in essence, said, Give up everything first, share it, then follow me. There are real needs among the poor, oppressed peoples of this earth. See them. Meet their need. Jesus proclaimed the good news

of the kingdom of God, which included service to the most desperate.

Lausanne Report on "Evangelism and Social Responsibility"

How are resistant areas effectively penetrated? Are there acceptable means to a society in general to demonstrate the love of God in Jesus Christ? Is it legitimate to delay proclamation until compassionate activity opens the door? Is the healing and feeding ministry of Jesus a model we must recover for twenty-first century missions among the unreached and those newly reached?

The Lausanne Covenant and the subsequent report called "Evangelism and Social Responsibility: An Evangelical Commitment" has much to say concerning this. Statement 5, "Christian Social Responsibility" of the Covenant, reads:

> We affirm that God is both the Creator and the Judge of all men. We therefore should share his concern for justice and reconciliation throughout human society and for the liberation of men and women from every kind of oppression. Because men and women are made in the image of God, every person, regardless of race, religion, colour, culture, class, sex or age, has an intrinsic dignity because of which he or she should be respected and served, not exploited. Here too we express penitence both for our neglect and for having sometimes regarded evangelism and social concern as mutually exclusive. Although reconciliation with other people is not reconciliation with God, nor is social action evangelism, nor is political liberation salvation, nevertheless we affirm that evangelism and socio-political involvement are both part of our Christian duty. For both are necessary expressions of our doctrines of God and man, our love for our neighbor and our obedience to Jesus Christ. The message of salvation implies also a message of judgment upon every form of alienation, oppression and discrimination, and we should not be afraid to denounce evil and injustice wherever they exist. When people receive Christ they are born again into his kingdom and must seek not only to exhibit but also to spread its righteousness in the midst of an unrighteous world. The salvation we claim should be transforming us in the totality of our personal and social responsibilities. Faith

without works is dead.[159]

Some argue that if evangelicals are to retain their commitment to evangelism, they should not engage in the social/political arena. The fear is that if we are committed to both, one is bound to suffer. However, Jesus both preached and cared for the needs of the people he touched. He challenged the religious political system and brought the message of God's kingdom and human's need of repentance.

Jesus struck a remarkable balance between evangelism and social action. But is there a priority between the two? The delegates at Lausanne seemed to think so. So do I. It is fundamental to affirm that "of all the tragic needs of human beings none is greater than their alienation from the Creator and the terrible reality of eternal death for those who refuse to repent and believe."[160] But along with proclaiming the love of God in Jesus Christ, one cannot escape the obligation to love one's neighbor. John Stott explains this well:

> Here then are two instructions of Jesus—a great compassion "love your neighbor" and a great commission "go and make disciples." What is the relation between the two? Some of us behave as if we thought them identical, so that if we share the Gospel with somebody, we consider we have completed our responsibility to love him. But no. The Great Commission neither explains, nor exhausts, nor supersedes the Great Compassion ... If we truly love our neighbor we shall without doubt share with him the good news of Jesus. How can we possibly claim to love him if we know the Gospel but keep it from him? Equally, however, if we truly love our neighbor we shall not stop with evangelism. Our neighbor is neither a bodiless soul that we should love only his soul, nor a soulless body that we should care for its welfare alone, nor even a body-soul isolated from society. God created man, who is my neighbor, a body-soul-in-community.[161]

Jesus teaches this in the Sermon on the Mount. He says we are salt

---

159   "The Lausanne Covenant." *Lausanne Committee for World Evangelization.* Lausanne: The Lausanne Commission, 1974. 2

160   "The Pattaya Statement." *Consultation on World Evangelism.* Pattaya, 1980.

161   John R.W. Stott, *Christian Mission in the Modern World* (Downers Grove: Inter-Varsity Press, 1975), 29–30.

and light. Salt permeates society and preserves it. Light reveals truth and goodness. Salt clearly represents our role in society. Light represents the proclamation of the Gospel both in word and deed. The church has modeled this in history. "Motivated by love for human beings in need, the early Christians went everywhere preaching the Word of God, because nothing has such a humanizing influence as the Gospel."[162]

Relationship of Evangelism and Social Responsibility

In the past century, the liberal wing of the church focused mainly on justice issues apart from proclaiming the message of salvation. The evangelical community shied away from social action for fear of neglecting the message and accusations of identifying with the liberals. There was infrequently a healthy balance.

But another problem surfaced. We forgot about those who never heard about Jesus and our service remained toward those who were served over and over. We forgot that the Great Commission would some day become the Great Completion.

The evangelical church has viewed the relationship between evangelism and social responsibility in three ways.

1. Social activity as a *consequence* of evangelism. Evangelism is the means by which God brings people to new birth, and their new life manifests itself in the service of others. Paul wrote, "Faith expresses itself in love" (Galatians 5:6). James says, "I will show you my faith through my good deeds" (James 2:18). We can even go on to say that social responsibility is more than just the consequence of evangelism; it is one of its principle aims. Ephesians 2:10 says, "He has created us anew in Christ Jesus, so that we can do the good things he planned for us long ago."

2. Social activity can be a *bridge* to evangelism. Social activity can break down barriers to direct evangelism. Tangible acts of love and service build bridges. Loving acts, such as responses to natural disasters, can indeed open people's hearts to hear the message of Christ. Recently, Mission India responded to those devastated by the tsunami in southern India. During the first phase of providing relief materials, the distribution of food and basic necessities changed the formerly closed attitudes of the

---

162   John R.W. Stott, *Involvement: Being a Responsible Christian in a Non-Christian Society* (Old Tappan: Revell, 1984), 42.

fishermen toward Christianity. Hundreds now embrace Christ, where only months before, open hostility existed.

3. Social activity accompanies evangelism as its *partner*. Jesus not only preached the Gospel, but also fed the hungry and healed the sick. Proclamation and service went hand in hand. His words explained his works and his works dramatized his words. Both were expressions of his love for people.

This of course applies to the unreached. We must recover the biblical practice of good works evangelism. But works of justice and freeing the oppressed certainly applies to our brothers and sisters caught in the backbreaking bonds of illiteracy. Therefore, I propose a fourth relationship between evangelism and social responsibility:

4. Social activity is our *responsibility* in the discipling process. Once a person has responded to the love of Christ, we are to help them grow up in their faith. Setting them free from the chains of sin and yet not removing the chains of illiteracy and thus oppression is not loving my neighbor.

In contrast to the short-term thinking of many churches today, and in a similar manner the Orality Movement (see chapter 5), effective strategies should be used combining both evangelism and social action. It is not enough to send short-term mission teams and build church buildings. Love must be expressed in tangible ways consistent with biblical direction. Micah 6:8 says, "The Lord has already told you what is good, and this is what he requires: to do what is right, to love mercy, and to walk humbly with your God." Christians have loved their neighbors in many ways. Recent church history can give us a glimpse of how others have done this.

Recent Examples of Evangelism and Social Responsibility

Recent church history reveals a rich heritage of evangelism linked with social activism. Even though:

the "official" churches were, by and large, indifferent; they showed little interest in the predicament of the poor in their own countries or the detrimental effects of colonial policies on the inhabitants of Europe's colonies. It was those touched by the awakenings who were moved to compassion by the plight of people exposed to the degrading conditions in slums and prisons, in coal-mining districts, on the American frontier, in West Indian plantations, and elsewhere. William Wilberforce, who launched a frontal attack on the practice of slavery in the British Empire, was an avowed evangelical. William Carey protested against sugar imports from West Indian plantations cultivated by slaves. Christian Blumhardt, one of the founding fathers of the Basel Mission, challenged the first group of Basel missionaries never to forget "how arrogant and scandalous the poor black people were for centuries . . . treated by people who call themselves Christians."[163]

John Wesley, in the eighteenth century, closely integrated the Gospel and social/political reform. "Christianity is essentially a social religion; to turn it into a solitary religion is indeed to destroy it."[164] "Wesley himself did more than talk about social reform. Among other things, he agitated for prison, liquor, and labour reform; set up loan funds for the poor; campaigned against the slave trade and smuggling; opened a dispensary and gave medicines to the poor; worked to solve unemployment; and personally gave considerable sums of money to persons in need."[165]

The Wesleyan revivals "reinforced a great passion for social concern and social justice. Not only Wesley, but also other evangelical forerunners . . . paved the way for several social reforms. These included the movement against slavery, campaigns for penal reform and the foundations of modern nursing."[166] Charles Finney (1792–1875) called slavery sin. "Where I have authority, I exclude slaveholders from communion, and I always will as long as I live."[167]

One of the finest examples of evangelistic social action is the pioneer of the modern Western Christian missionary movement.

---

163   David J. Bosch, *Transforming Mission: Paradigm Shifts in Theology of Mission* (New York: Orbis, 1991), 281.

164   John Wesley, *The Works of John Wesley*. Vol. V (London: John Manson, 1829), 296.

165   Howard A. Snyder, *The Problem of Wine Skins* (Downers Grove: Inter-Varsity Press, 1975), 172.

166   Jacob Thomas, *From Lausanne to Manila: Evangelical Social Thought* (Delhi: India Society for Promoting Christian Knowledge, 2003), 9.

167   Ibid., 10.

William Carey talked of a "worldly spirituality, with a strong emphasis on justice and love for one's fellows, as on love for God, marked the turning point of Indian culture from a downward to upward trend."[168] Vishal Mangalwadi relates the story of Carey's compassionate response to infanticide.

> In 1794, near Malda, Carey had his first horrifying experience of infanticide. He found the remains of an infant devoured by white ants after having been offered as a sacrifice. He could never be content after that with the mere telling of the story of a Savior who died for humanity, including little ones. Carey felt obligated to struggle to save their lives.

> Every winter at the Sagar *mela*, where the sea and the River Hooghly meet, children were pushed down the mud-banks into the sea to be either drowned or devoured by crocodiles, all in the fulfillment of vows their mothers had made. This was looked upon as a most holy sacrifice—giving to the Mother Ganges the fruit of their bodies for the sins of their souls. As Carey's concern for these victims of superstitious beastliness became known, he was asked by the British governor general to inquire into the numbers, nature, and reasons for infanticide. Carey said that he took this assignment with great readiness. His report resulted in the practice being outlawed. The moment of satisfaction came when Carey's group went to the Sagar *puja* (worship of the ocean) in 1804 to proclaim the story of God's own sacrifice. They found that due to administrative vigilance, not a single infant could be sacrificed to the goddess. What a victory: A wicked "religious" practice had been suppressed.[169]

Why have Christians responded in such a way? Yes, in obedience to Christ's instruction to be salt and light. But at a more basic level because of the Christian doctrine of humanity—that we are image bearers of the living God. Even though we are all fallen creatures, people still matter and are the center of God's plan of redemption. Evangelism and

---

168   Vishal and Ruth Mangalwadi, *The Legacy of William Carey* (Wheaton: Crossway Books, 1999), 25.
169   Ibid., 33.

social responsibility have walked hand-in-hand fulfilling the two Great Commandments.

This is not a new teaching, nor a new practice. But it must be recovered again as a vital tool in bringing the Gospel to those who have not yet heard. Literacy can play an important role.

Implications

The two Great Commandments of Jesus are to be the two great goals of his Church. Literacy, using Bible content primers, is an effective way to meet the core needs of the developing world, especially in India today. Light comes through God's Word. Wholeness in society comes by linking both truth and justice. The opportunity for sustained discipleship becomes a reality not only by imparting the ability to read the Word of God, but through bringing freedom from the oppressive bondage of illiteracy. Transformation is the goal.

Transformation is the change from a condition of human existence contrary to God's purpose to one in which people are able to enjoy fullness of life in harmony with God and others (John 10:10; Colossians 3:8–15; Ephesians 4:13). This transformation can only take place through the obedience of individuals and communities to the Gospel of Jesus Christ, whose power changes the lives of men and women by releasing them from guilt, power, and consequences of sin, enabling them to respond with love toward God and toward others (Romans 5:5), and making them "new creatures in Christ" (2 Corinthians 5:17).[170]

Literacy is a useful tool in this process.

---

170   Vinay Samuel and Christopher Sugden, *The Church in Response to Human Need* (Grand Rapids: Eerdmans, 1987).

Chapter 7
Literacy, Discipleship, and Development

Is discipleship limited to the spiritual dimension of the human being? If indeed this encapsulates Jesus' call to "make disciples," then perhaps the need for literacy in discipling the emerging church in India remains under question. There are few who would disagree that literacy is critical at least for church pastors and leaders. The ability to read the Bible is necessary at least for them. However, does not discipleship encompass the transformation of the whole person? This includes his relationships with others, his health, and his ability to take care of his own needs and provide for others. All transformation begins with spiritual change, but should not stop here. Biblical transformation and discipleship is "the process of restoration to God's intention of all that was broken when humanity rebelled against God at the fall."[171]

Chris Wright in an article on holistic mission in "Lausanne World Pulse" says:

> A full biblical understanding of the atonement goes far beyond personal guilt and individual forgiveness. That Jesus died in my place, bearing the guilt of my sin, is of course the most glorious liberating truth. That we should long for others to know this truth and be saved and forgiven by placing their sins on the crucified Savior in repentance and faith is a most energizing motive for evangelism. But there is more in the biblical theology of the cross than individual salvation, and there is more to biblical mission than evangelism. The Gospel is good news for the whole creation (Mark 16:15, cf. Ephesians 3:10). Pointing out the wider dimensions of God's redemptive mission (and therefore of our committed holistic participation in God's mission) is not "watering down" the

---

171   Robert Mofitt, "Transformation: Dream or Reality?" *Evangelical Mission Quarterly*, vol. 41, no. 4 (October 2005), 490.

Gospel of personal salvation. Rather, we set that precious good news for the individual firmly and affirmatively within its full biblical context of all that God has achieved, and will finally complete, through the cross of Christ for the whole of creation.[172]

A disciple is one who is in the process of transformation. "Ultimately, all that will exist in the new, redeemed creation will be there because of the cross. Conversely, all that will not be there (suffering, tears, sin, Satan, sickness, oppression, injustice, corruption, decay, and death) will not be there because they will have been defeated by the cross."[173]

Many evangelical voices are now articulating a holistic vision. Charles Taber says, "Every human being, *all* human beings—are created in the image and likeness of God and therefore possess an inalienable and innate dignity that no one can rightly take away on any pretext whatever."[174] Human dignity is clearly denied to those who remain illiterate. How is it we can disciple those who cannot read and yet be content to leave them in the state of "social, economic, political, and religious systems marked by injustice, exploitation, and oppression?"[175]

The problem is we do not understand what it is like to be illiterate. Frank Laubach makes a comparison between the lack of understanding illiteracy to our lack of understanding starvation. He is critical of the tremendous war against disease fought by medical missions without a corresponding war against starvation. Medicine has extended life spans across the globe resulting in ever-increasing populations. All of us understand the effects and pain of disease and so sending medical missionaries to bring healing is a natural loving response. But Christians have not sent corresponding agricultural specialists to increase farm production to feed the increasing populations. The reason, according to Laubach is *"we do not understand starvation."*[176] This is because few have

---

172   Chris Wright, "Re-affirming Holistic Mission: A Cross-Centered Approach in All Areas of Life" *Lausanne World Pulse*, October 2005, 11.

173   Ibid.

174   Charles R. Taber, "In the Image of God: The Gospel and Human Rights," *International Bulletin of Missionary Research*, July 2002, 102.

175   Vinay Samuel and Christopher Sugden, "Transformation: The Church in Response to Human Need," *The Consultation on the Church in Response to Human Need*: Wheaton Illinois, June 1983, 4.

176   Frank C. Laubach, *War of Amazing Love* (Westwood: Fleming H. Revell Co., 1965), 18.

come in contact with people who are actually starving. However, health is another matter. It is easy to empathize when friends die of disease. All people understand misery. A war must be waged against it. But starvation is seldom if ever a problem in the West. In fact, the opposite is true. Waistlines are swelling.

The same goes for literacy. *There is little understanding of illiteracy.* Some reason that if the good news comes, illiteracy does not really matter or will take care of itself. But this ignores the crippling effects of illiteracy. They do not go away even after a person has responded to the gracious call of the Lord Jesus on their life.

> In the underdeveloped areas of the world, the educated people own the land because they write the deeds, and make the laws, and judge in the court; they mint the money, control the army, run businesses and governments. The illiterates possess next to nothing; indeed, they are in debt their entire lives. They don't know how much they owe; they only realize that the debt is staggering. The one aching desire of their hearts is to rise from their misery to the level of the educated people—and they know (even if we don't) that the only means of escape for them and their children is through the doorway which opens up a new world. *This doorway is literacy!*[177]

It is not enough to reason that providing spiritual nurture is enough for discipling the emerging church in India. Unlike church growth in China and South Korea in the last century, India's growth remains stagnant (at least according to census data). One significant difference between these nations is the low literacy rate remaining in India. Church growth cannot sustain without a Bible reading leadership and will be weak and poor without a Bible reading membership.

Lamin Sanneh comments on a paradox in the ministry of David Livingstone's service in Africa. Livingstone was a stalwart defender of the virtues of primitive tribes, yet at the same time he justified colonial rule. In this context he says, "Livingstone was prepared to trust the vernacular Bible to usher in the kingdom of God and so thorough was his faith in that agency that he wished to relinquish it into the hands of native Africans without European superintendency."[178] In order to trust

---

177   Ibid., 90.
178   Lamin Sanneh, *Translating the Message: The Missionary Impact on Culture* (Maryknoll:

the vernacular Bible, assumptions are made that a person can actually read the book and remove the blinders of illiteracy. Sanneh then quotes Livingstone: "When converts are made from heathenism by modern missionaries, it becomes an interesting question whether their faith possesses the elements of permanence, or is it only an exotic too tender for self-propagation when the fostering care of the foreign cultivator is withdrawn. If neither habits of self-reliance are cultivated, nor opportunities given for the exercise of that virtue, the most promising converts are apt to become like spoiled children."[179] Certainly, one of the key elements in fostering self-reliance is the skill of reading. Self-reliance needs to be a biblical discipleship objective.

Human Development and Literacy

Human development and literacy are closely linked. The United Nations has initiated much of the work in this area. Literacy is stated as a basic human right deriving from the Universal Declaration of Human Rights in 1948. "The 2004–2005 UNESCO planning document makes the promotion of 'education as a fundamental human right in accordance with the Universal Declaration of Human Rights' the first contextual parameter for its work."[180]

In a report issued by the United Nations entitled "Human Development Report 1990," they identify the "three essential elements of human life—longevity, knowledge and decent living standards."[181] Longevity has to do with life expectancy at birth. "The importance of life expectancy lies in the common belief that a long life is valuable in itself and in the fact that various indirect benefits (such as adequate nutrition and good health) are closely associated with higher life expectancy."[182] Knowledge is fundamentally rooted in literacy. "Literacy is a person's first step in learning and knowledge-building, so literacy figures are essential in any measurement of human development."[183] They then go on to say that for basic human development, "literacy deserves the

---

Orbis Books, 1989), 108–109.

179   Ibid., 109.

180   "Literacy: An Evolving Concept," *United Nations Literacy Decade 2003–2012.* Chapter 3, 2. http://portal.unesco.org/education/ev.php?URL_ID=13206&URL_DO=DO.

181   *Human Development Report 1990*, United Nations Development Programme, 12.

182   Ibid.

183   Ibid.

clearest emphasis."[184] This third component of human development is the need to earn a decent living. Income is the best indicator at this time. All three of these indicators of development are strongly correlated with literacy. These "essential elements of human life" should not be neglected nor separated from the discipleship process. Obedience to Christ's commands is both for the discipler and the disciple. A discipler cannot be content with his or her converts continuing to live in squalor, unable to improve their living conditions due to illiteracy. The disciple cannot be content with only being spoon fed God's Word from leaders in most cases who are themselves in the same predicament. Let us take a closer look at the three essentials of human life.

Longevity

In a study quoted earlier relating to assessing Israelite literacy, Meir Bar-Ilan examines the relationship of life expectancy to literacy in eight nations as of 1974. The table below is the result of his study.

	Netherlands	USA	Romania	Brazil	Algeria	China	India	Gabon
Literate in percent	98	98	98	61	30	25	28	12
Infant Mortality (1000/year)	11	18	35	94	128	65	139	227
Life expectancy (years)	74	71	68	61	51	62	50	41

Table 7.1 Contemporary Nations—3 aspects 15

He concluded from his research that the "higher the literacy rate, the lower the number of infant deaths and the higher the life expectancy."[185] He used this along with several other measuring tools to assess Israelite literacy at the time of Christ.

Bar-Ilan's research is supported by the international development community. Amartya Sen, the winner of the Nobel Prize in economics in 1998, published a book entitled *Development as Freedom*. In it he compares infant mortality and adult literacy in India and Sub-Saharan Africa. The following table reflects his analysis:

---

184   Ibid.
185   Ibid.

India and Sub-Saharan Africa: Selected Comparisons (1991)

	Infant mortality rate comparisons			Adult literacy rate comparisons		
	Region	Population (millions)	Infant mortality rate (per 1,000 live births)	Region	Population	Adult literacy rate (female/male)
INDIA	India	846.3	80	India	846.3	39/64
"Worst" three Indian states	Orissa	31.7	124	Rajasthan	44	20/55
	Madhya Pradesh	66.2	117	Bihar	86.4	23/52
	Uttar Pradesh	139.1	97	Uttar Pradesh	139.1	25/56
"Worst" district of each of the "worst" Indian states	Ganjam (Orissa)	3.2	164	Barmer (Rajasthan)	1.4	8/37
	Tikamgarh (Madhya Pradesh	0.9	152	Kishanganj (Bihar)	1	10/33
	Hardoi (Uttar Pradesh)	2.7	129	Bahraich (Uttar Pradesh)	2.8	11/36
"Worst" three countries of Sub-Saharan Africa	Mali	8.7	161	Burkina Faso	9.2	10/31
	Mozambique	16.1	149	Sierra Leone	4.3	12/35
	Guinea-Bissau	1	148	Benin	4.8	17/35
SUB-SAHARAN AFRICA	Sub-Saharan Africa	488.9	104	Sub-Saharan Africa	488.9	40/63

Table 7.2 India and Sub-Saharan Africa: Selected Comparisons (1991) [17]

Sen makes the observation that "there is no country in the sub-Saharan Africa—or indeed the world—where estimated infant mortality rates are as high as in the district of Ganjam in Orissa, or where the adult female literacy rate is as low as in the district of Barmer in Rajasthan."[186] In the same section in this book, Sen says that "about half of all Indian children . . . are chronically undernourished."[187] The one problem that both India and sub-Saharan Africa have in common is the "persistence of endemic illiteracy—a feature that, like low life expectancy, sets South Asia and sub-Saharan Africa apart from the rest of the world."[188] Sen labels these three features of deprivation: premature mortality, undernourishment, and illiteracy. This is consistent with the findings of Bar-Ilan.

186   Ibid., 101.
187   Ibid., 102.
188   Ibid., 103.

Sen also links female illiteracy with another disturbing problem in India today: gender bias in child survival. "Female literacy . . . is found to have an unambiguous and statistically significant reducing impact on under-five mortality." This is especially critical in India as the female child survival rate is considerably less than the male child. According to the 2001 census data, there are 933 females for every 1,000 males. In the Union Territory Daman and Diu, there are only 710 females for every 1,000 males. Sen concludes that "higher levels of female literacy and labor force participation being strongly associated with lower levels of relative female disadvantage in child survival."[189] The state of Kerala has the highest literacy rate in India at 91 percent. It is no coincidence that it also has the highest ratio of female to male children—1,058 to 1,000.[190]

Child survival and longevity deserve our concern and action. These basic elements of human existence are rooted in the value of each and every person as image bearers of our Creator. Literacy is a key component in valuing every human life.

Knowledge

"Education, in the present day context, is perhaps the single most important means for individuals to improve personal endowments, build capability levels, overcome constraints and, in the process, enlarge their available set of opportunities and choices for a sustained improvement in well-being."[191] The government of India then goes on to say, "Lower fertility, infant and child mortality rates; better nutritional, hygiene and health status of children, reproductive health and empowerment of women; social mobility and political freedom, all have visible linkages with educational attainments of people. It is, undoubtedly, a basic component of human development."[192]

UNICEF published a report in 1999 entitled "The State of the World's Children." They assert that the right of education is a "matter of morality, justice and economic sense. There is an unmistakable correlation between education and mortality rates, especially child mortality."[193] Kerala is again used as an example of how education makes

---

189   Ibid., 197.
190   India Census Data, 2001. http://www.censusindia.net/t_00_006.html. http://www.censusindia.net/religiondata/Summary%20Christians.pdf.
191   "National Human Development Report 2001," *Planning Commission Government of India*, March 2002, 48.
192   Ibid.
193   Carol Bellamy, *The State of the World's Children 1999* (United Nations Children's

a huge difference. There "infant mortality is the lowest in the entire developing world—and the fertility rate is the lowest in India."[194]

The same report discussed the broad social benefits of educating girls, noting: (1) The more educated a mother is, the more infant and child mortality is reduced. (2) Children of more educated mothers tend to be better nourished and suffer less from illness. (3) Children (and particularly daughters) of more educated mothers are more likely to be educated themselves and become literate. (4) The more education women have, the later they tend to marry and the fewer children they tend to have. (5) Educated women are less likely to die in childbirth. (6) The more educated a woman is, the more likely she is to have opportunities and life choices and avoid exploitation by her family or social situation. (7) Educated women are more likely to be receptive to, participate in, and influence development initiatives and send their own daughters to school. (8) Educated women are more likely to play a role in political and economic decision-making at community, regional, and national levels.[195] UNESCO makes similar assertions concerning the benefits of literacy. They say that a person born in a literate family (1) has a better chance to survive infancy and acquire the foundation for learning; (2) is more likely to go to school and get the parental support to stay there; (3) tends to marry later and have fewer and healthier children; (4) is more likely to find qualified jobs; (5) is more likely to participate in democratic life; and (6) is more interested in caring for the environment.[196] In a doctoral project with the southern state of Tamil Nadu in India as the research area, P. Kamala indicates, "Ignorance is directly related to illiteracy and illiteracy breeds poverty. There is a definite relationship between illiteracy and poverty."[197] The World Bank has defined poverty as an "expenditure under a dollar a day."[198] In the next chapter of this book, it will become evident that the majority of illiterates fall under this threshold of absolute poverty. Lack

---

Fund, 1999), 7.

194   Ibid., 8.

195   Ibid., 52.

196   *UNESCO and Education*, Paris: The Media Team Education Sector, UNESCO. Accessed. Available from *unesdoc.unesco.org/images/0012/001289/128951e.pdf. 1*

197   P. Kamala, "Role of Adult Education in Rural Development: A Study in the Selected Villages of Two Districts in Tamil Nadu." University of Madras for the Degree of Doctor of Philosophy, 1993, 24.

198   Mani Shankar Aiyar, "India File: Poverty in China and India" *Washington Times*, January 1, 2003.

of knowledge—the minimal basics of reading and writing—results in poverty, disease, and the inability of the person and their progeny to move beyond this trap. Literacy as a tool of discipleship is an act of love toward those ignored or mistreated.

Decent Living Standards

There is a strong correlation between illiteracy and poverty in all the literature. According to UNICEF, "Without education, children are virtually *condemned* to a life of poverty, ill health and general lack of material and intellectual well-being" (emphasis mine).[199] The choice of the word *condemned* is penetrating. If indeed this word is accurate, we who are educated are in the role of judge and in a real sense "inflict a penalty upon" or "doom" the illiterate child.[200] Conversion without demonstrated loving concern for the person's well-being does not fulfill the Great Compassion, to love our neighbor.

Child labor illustrates the link between illiteracy and poverty. According to the authors of *Child Labour, A Global Challenge*, "Poverty seems to be one of the most dominant reasons" for child labor.[201] Poverty is supplemented by other socio-economic factors, these being a "high degree of illiteracy and ignorance of the parents."[202] When are poverty and its most pervasive cause of illiteracy worthwhile addressing as a holistic discipleship matter? When children are forced to work? "Illiteracy persist[s] predominantly in child labour."[203] Table 7.3 is cited by the authors as evidence of illiteracy among child laborers. This data is from the 1981 census of India.

The correlation between illiteracy and child labor is hard to deny. Child labor and poor living standards go hand-in-hand. "Literacy tends to make an individual self-sufficient."[204] Decent living standards are difficult to obtain for those whose eyes are blind to the printed page.

---

199 "UNICEF Says India Must Improve Basic Education," Reuters, December 8, 1998, India Literacy Project.

200 David B. Guralink, ed., *Webster's New World Dictionary of the American Language* (New York: Simon and Schuster, 1982), 295.

201 Tapan Kumar Shandilya and Shakeel Ahmad Khan, *Child Labour, A Global Challenge* (New Delhi: Deep & Deep Publications, 2003), 13.

202 Ibid., 14.

203 Ibid., 60.

204 David R. Olson and Nancy Torrance, *The Making of Literate Societies* (Malden: Blackwell Publishers, 2001), 290.

Gender-Based Distribution of Child Workers by Educational Levels, Rural and Urban Areas

Sl. No.	Educational Level	Male		Female	
		Rural	Urban	Rural	Urban
1	Illiterate	5,342,133	469,128	3,117,111	195,067
		79.75%	63.47%	88.93%	77.25%
2	Literate (without educational level)	688,782	113,162	195,723	27,572
		10.28%	15.31%	55.80%	10.92%
3	Primary	574,730	127,725	168,601	25,241
		8.58%	17.28%	4.81%	10.00%
4	Middle	85,659	25,681	22,721	4,132
		1.28%	3.47%	6.50%	1.64%
5	Matriculation/ Secondary	6,920	3,180	973	472
		0.10%	0.43%	0.03%	0.19%
6	Higher Secondary/ Intermediate/ Pre-University	437	221	32	22
		0.01%	0.03%	0.00%	0.00%
7	Non-Technical Diploma or Certificate not equal to Degree	36	26	16	5
		0.00%	0.00%	0.00%	0.00%
8	Technical Diploma or Certificate not equal to Degree	47	8	9	5
		0.00%	0.00%	0.00%	0.00%
9	Total Workers	6,698,743	739,102	3,505,185	253,514
		100.00%	100.00%	100.00%	100.00%

Table 7.3 Child Workers by Education, Urban and Rural 34

Illiterates generally live below the absolute poverty line established by the United Nations (earning less than $1 per day). In the case of Mission India's work, the reader can see below that of the 73,915 graduates of the literacy program over the period from 2002–2005, the average income at the start of the program was 35 rupees or $0.77. This is significantly below the poverty line. After just one year of literacy training, income increased by 57 percent. In our own work, we see a direct relationship to decent living standards and literacy.

MISSION INDIA
Income Change Resulting from Literacy

Year	Total Graduates from Annual Reports	Average Daily Income at Start of Program in Rupees	Average Daily Income measured after Literacy in Rupees	Percentage Change
2002	20,108	37.85	55.44	46%
2003	20,364	33.2	51.13	54%
2004	33,443	34.17	56.65	66%
TOTALS	**73,915**	**35**	**55**	**57%**

Table 7.4 Income Change Resulting from Literacy

Many take advantage of this severe handicap and see that the illiterate remains oppressed. We need to see part of our role in discipleship as being an advocate for those who "have never had a delegate anywhere, have been voiceless, the silent victims, the forgotten men, mutely submitting since the dawn and before the dawn of history. It is a human weakness not to recognize suffering until we hear a cry, and these illiterates could not make their cry reach the rest."[205] We have the blessed responsibility of not just telling them about Jesus, but helping restore the wholeness that was lost and contributes daily to their brief and unhealthy lives, their ignorance and thus exploitation and their inability to earn enough money to meet their daily needs. Literacy needs to become an important component of discipling efforts, especially in India today.

Literacy and Discipleship Today

Discipleship is not simply the point in time at which conversion takes place. Discipleship has a definite beginning, but the process continues. In looking at the role of literacy in discipling the emerging church in India, it is important to recognize the benefits literacy brings at the beginning of the process. Literacy opens the door to communities resistant to traditional approaches to evangelism. This was illustrated in the example of V. David. The tribal group he approached resisted his evangelistic efforts with death threats. But when he asked them if they wanted to learn to read, they welcomed him into the community. Frank Laubach also makes the

---

205   Frank C. Laubach, *India Shall Be Literate* (Fabri Press, 2007), 5.

same observation in an address entitled *Literacy and Evangelism*. "We have discovered that where non-Christians will not listen to straight preaching, they welcome you if you teach them, because they want to learn to read.... Literacy is the entering wedge."[206]

Why does literacy open the door to discipleship? Ruth Warren says in her booklet on literacy, "Among the incentives are economic pressure, social prestige, political curiosity, civic competency, improvement of living standards. But probably the three most powerful motives are letter-writing, escape from the money lender and other cheats, and access to the religious books."[207] The simple tool of literacy is a door opener for evangelism. For example, Mission India has been conducting literacy classes in India for over 20 years, first starting in 1985. The statistics from 2002 through 2006 are reflected in the table below.

MISSION INDIA LITERACY GRADUATES

Year	Graduates	Commitments to Christ	Baptisms
2002	18,134	9,473	1,427
2003	21,844	7,425	1,695
2004	32,101	11,655	3,976
2005	53,530	14,693	5,384
2006	85,203	26,793	13,413
TOTALS	**210,812**	**70,039**	**25,895**
PERCENTAGE OF GRADUATES		**33.2%**	**12.3%**

Table 7.5 Percentage of Literacy Learners Making Commitments to Christ

As you can see, one third of the learners graduating from this literacy program have committed their lives to Jesus Christ. These learners are almost entirely from Hindu and Muslim communities. Literacy training serves the illiterate community and is valued. Like Frank Laubach's work among Muslims in Pakistan,[208] Mission India finds a similar openness among Muslim communities to literacy and the Gospel in Hyderabad, Bhopal, and West Bengal.

---

206   Frank C. Laubach, "Literacy as Evangelism," *Annual Meeting of Foreign Mission Conference January 1950*, Buck Hills Falls, Pennsylvania (New York: Mohican Press, 1950), 2.

207   Ruth Ure Warren, *Literacy* (London: Edinburgh House Press, 1955), 19.

208   Laubach, *Literacy as Evangelism*.

Literacy is a very useful and effective tool in making disciples especially in gaining an audience with an otherwise resistant community. But illiteracy is also the plight of the emerging church in India. In the next chapter, we will review the data that supports this conclusion. Literacy opens the door to resistant communities and is useful in maturing new disciples. One of the primary motives of new believers for literacy is so they can read the Bible for themselves. "Christians are taught to read so the Bible and other literature will enrich their faith and make them more effective Christians. Paul's letters were originally written as a means of communicating with new churches. The same need exists today."[209]

A looming threat to the emerging church is syncretism and reversion back to former religions. David Mason says, "In nations with high illiteracy, literacy education is a stabilizing force in the church. Many African converts who were not literate enough to continue reading the Bible drifted back into paganism. Literacy is a powerful instrument in the preservation and the growth of a Christian outlook on life."[210] Ruth Warren likewise says, "A church without a Bible dies. It happened in history. It happens today. To be sure, a preacher can preach, but how much can a congregation remember? After all, individual access to the Scriptures is the basis of Protestantism."[211] Considering the research done for this book, it is necessary to ask what it is the preacher is preaching given that 70 percent of those leading the churches cannot read the Bible for themselves.

The importance of the printed page to human history and human development is foundational. It was the written Word of God in the vernacular of the common person that called the corrupt church to account and started a reformation that has shaped Western civilization ever since. It is this written Word that is the basis for transformational discipleship. Loving our neighbors, especially brothers and sisters in Christ, includes more than the spiritual conversion of oppressed and exploited peoples. The Great Compassion demands they be freed from the shackles of ignorance so they can more truly reflect the beauty of being an image bearer of the divine.

Literacy transforms resistant peoples to becoming receptive to hear—and in many cases receive—the Good News. And literacy

---

209   David E. Mason, *Reaching the Silent Billion: The Opportunity of Literacy Missions* (Grand Rapids: Zondervan, 1967), 30.

210   Ibid., 20.

211   Warren, 9.

strengthens new believers to become lifelong self-sufficient yet interdependent disciples of Jesus.

Implications

Illiteracy is like being in prison. The crime is birth. Hindus would call it karma or repayment for sins from a past life. The penalty: a shortened life span, high infant mortality and children who have to work instead of going to school, exploitation and oppression, absolute poverty (not the relative poverty we know in the West). The list goes on. And for followers of Jesus Christ, there is the high probability of syncretism leading to dangerous heresy and often the road back to paganism. Bringing literacy is a practical and important expression of love to our neighbor, as we love ourselves.

Chapter 8
Measuring Discipleship

The focus of this book is the emerging church in India. The research itself comes out of the ministries of a church planting ministry in India. In order to assess the literacy rate among the emerging churches in India, two surveys on literacy and discipleship were conducted among two distinct groups. The first survey was among grass-roots level church planters from the state of Andhra Pradesh. The second survey was conducted among church and mission leaders from across India representing 20 different states. These first two surveys used a written questionnaire read and filled out by those completing the survey. The second phase of this research consisted of interviews among new believers, literate and illiterate, in two distinct locations, one in an urban slum and one in a rural community. The purpose of this second phase was to see if there were measurable behavioral differences relating to discipleship between literate and illiterate believers. The interview questions were asked by an interviewer and recorded as answered by the respondents.

All of the research for this section of the book was conducted through the work of an indigenous mission in India. The objective of this organization is to assist Indian Christians in planting reproducing churches in a systematic and measurable way.

This entity works with approximately 1,000 partner organizations in India, including denominations, independent churches, mission and Christian social service organizations with a church planting focus. An example of this ministry's mission statement follows:

- Assists—It serves Indian Christians, provides funds and training to them, without stifling their independence or exercising authority over them. Indian Christians, not foreigners and not Western staff, are God's chosen agents whom he has gifted to establish churches in India.

- Indian Christians—Christian believers in India are the ones God has called and gifted to plant churches most effectively in India today. Indian Christians are under the authority of and sent by indigenous Indian churches or mission organizations.
- Planting—Churches are living spiritual organisms that start from seed, the Word of God. Churches grow, mature, bear fruit, and multiply, much like the life cycle of a living plant. This organization assists Indian Christians in the beginning and most challenging phase of the church growth process, the initial planting and establishing of new churches.
- Reproducing—Churches are living spiritual organisms that reproduce their own kind, using their own resources to bear fruit through daughter churches. The most effective way India can be reached with the Gospel is if new churches learn to reproduce themselves without depending on foreign assistance.
- Churches—Churches are local fellowships of Christ's disciples, who meet together regularly under local leadership for worship, prayer, mutual edification, sacraments, service to the community and outreach. Each Indian partner organization follows its own operational definition of "church" and this organization seeks to honor those definitions.
- Systematic—Church planting assistance is not given haphazardly or merely in response to chance relationships or local circumstances, but with a goal to saturate all of India with churches, geographically and ethnically, so that every community and every people group has a growing church in their midst.
- Measurable—They expect Indian partners and staff to measure and report what God is doing through their efforts.

Emerging Churches in India

What is the emerging church in India today? It is comprised of the poor, oppressed peoples of India who respond to the proclamation of the Good News. Most of the church growth in India today is among these peoples: the dalits or untouchables, the tribals, the scheduled and unscheduled castes.[212] The emerging church in India is not the same as

---

212   David B. Barrett, *World Christian Encyclopedia*, Volume 1 (New York: Oxford University Press, 2001), 368–371. A review of the data on church and denominational growth reveals significant growth among these communities. I have observed that this is the case after becoming familiar with a broad range of mission organizations.

the emergent church movement in the Western world. Andy Crouch, in an article in *Christianity Today*, describes the Western emergent church as "frequently urban, disproportionately young, overwhelmingly white, and very new—few have been in existence for more than five years."[213] He then describes the emerging church as "works in progress, often startlingly improvisational in their approach to everything from worship to leadership to preaching to prayer. Like their own members, they live in the half-future tense of the young, oriented toward their promise rather than their past."[214] This is *not* a description of the emerging church in India. There, it is young and old alike, with almost all new believers. The membership of this emerging church was set free from idolatry, animistic beliefs and Islam. Where India is prospering financially, the Gospel does not take root as easily. It is the same as in any developed nation. Unfortunately with prosperity comes a sense of independence and pride, which resist repentance and surrender to the Lord Jesus.

Strategies include a grass-roots church planter training program called the Institute of Community Transformation or ICT. Each institute or school consists of ten students each in a full-time two-year program. No campus exists for the training of church planters. In the early days of this program, in the mid-1980s, students came to Chennai to attend classes. However, it was soon discovered that bringing them to a central location in a major metropolitan area had several negative consequences. First, there was a higher dropout rate than expected. Second, students were less eager to return to their villages and desired to stay in the urban areas. Finally, the students would lose contact with those they were ministering to while in class for a two-month period. Because of this, a decision was made to host only church planter training schools in the areas the church planters live. These are called "on-site schools" in contrast to schools that are campus centered. It became the mission or churches' responsibility to provide the space for the students to live in while attending residential classes. And since they were studying in their immediate areas, they could continue to serve in the villages on weekends even while they were attending classes during the week.

The average educational level of these students is 10th grade, with the following minimum literacy requirement: reading 30 words per minute with comprehension, writing 10 words per minute, and the ability to do basic mathematical functions. The students are in the classroom one-third

213   Andy Crouch, "The Emergent Mystique," *Christianity Today*, November 2004.
214   Ibid.

of the time (eight months total or four two-month terms) and doing field work the other two-thirds of the time (sixteen months). The objective is that each church planter will plant a minimum of two new churches each with ten baptized believers by the end of the two-year training program. Without going into a detailed explanation of the program, the graduates actually plant an average of 4.5 churches during their two-year training period, averaging 361 graduates per year over the last five years. It is with a group of these graduates that the research for this book on the literacy rate in the emerging church in India began.

Survey 1—Grass-Roots Church Planters

In October of 2003, an alumni conference hosted 100 students who graduated from the two-year church planter training program. This was conducted in Hyderabad, and the graduates were from the state of Andhra Pradesh. The literacy survey was handed out at this three-day conference and collected before the participants left. The questions asked are as follows:

1. Of the new believers coming to Christ in the churches and prayer cells you have planted, what percentage of them do you consider functionally literate?
2. What percentage of the believers in the new churches planted can read the Bible with understanding?
3. In your opinion, what is the literacy rate among people coming to Christ across India?
4. What level of importance does literacy play (the ability to read the Bible with understanding) in the discipling of new believers?
5. What level of importance does literacy play (the ability to read the Bible with understanding) in the maturing of the emerging church in India?
6. What percentage of the congregations in the emerging churches in your work has teachers/leaders who can read the Word of God with understanding?

This was the first attempt to understand the condition of literacy in the emerging church from the perspective of those trained in one language group (Telegu) and in one state in India. Of the 100 people who received the forms, 82 responded. The estimated literacy rate of the new believers was expected. Questions 1 and 2 addressed this matter specifically. The following charts help us understand the results of these two questions.

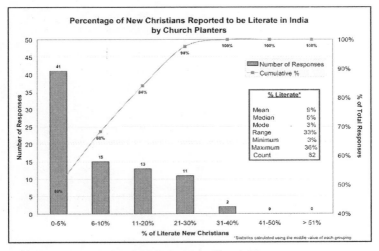

Table 8.1 Response to Survey Question 1 by Church Planters

Table 8.1 represents the responses to the perceived literacy rate among new believers in the new churches planted by the church planters. In calculating the responses, the mid-point of each range was defined by the specific number response. For example, 50 percent of the respondents indicated that they believe the literacy rate of the new Christians is between 0 and 5 percent. The mid-point of that response for the sake of analysis is 3 percent. The same applies to each choice available to the respondent. The most frequent response or mode is a 3 percent literacy rate. The middle value or median is 5 percent and the average literacy rate or mean is 9 percent. These grass-roots level workers estimate the average literacy rate of the emerging church is less than 10 percent. This data supports the underlying premise of this book that the literacy rate is low among new believers in India today. It is interesting to note that this literacy rate is similar to the literacy rate of the early church and consistent with the research cited in chapter 4 of this book.

The second question is more specific. Reading the Bible requires a higher level of literacy than being able to read the sign on a bus or to sign one's name. It is also significant in discipleship, assuming that the ability to read the Bible is useful for spiritual growth and ongoing discipleship.

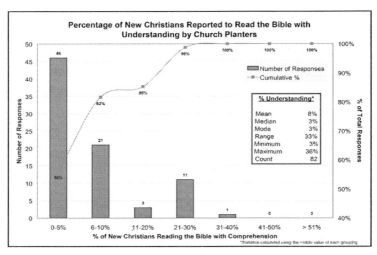

Table 8.2 Response to Survey Question 2 by Church Planters

As visible in Table 8.2 above, both the median and mode are at 3 percent with the average at 8 percent. This is lower than the perceived literacy rate in question 1, which is expected. The ability of new believers to read the Bible is very limited—less than 5 percent—in this group represented by 82 church planters in Andhra Pradesh. There is a difference in the operational definition of literacy assumed by the church planters on this question. Bible reading is perceived to require a higher level of literacy than a basic level of literacy assumed in question 1.

Question 3 asks the graduates' perception of the literacy rate of people coming to Christ across India. As pointed out earlier, the average educational level of church planters in this program is 10th grade. Their perspective on all of India will be somewhat limited, since most only speak the state language, Telegu, and will not have traveled outside their immediate area. (It is important to note that the survey was translated into Telegu so the respondents could read and answer the questions). However, their perception is worth noting. These former students believe the literacy rate in other parts of India is generally higher than in the regions they are working. The average response was a 14 percent literacy rate as compared with an 8 percent estimate in their immediate ministry area. According to the Census of India 2001, the literacy rate in Andhra Pradesh is 60.5

percent, which is slightly lower than the national average of 64.8 percent.[215] The response is consistent with the census data but could also reflect a view that those outside the immediate area are better off on average.

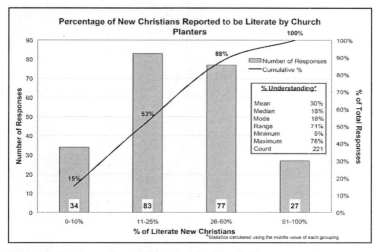

Table 8.3 Response to Survey Question 3 by Church Planters

The fourth and fifth questions concerning the perception of these students on the importance of reading the Bible for discipleship is overwhelmingly "very important." Question 4 was worded, "What level of importance does literacy play (the ability to read the Bible with understanding) in the discipling of new believers?" Seventy-one of the 83 respondents indicated that it was "very important." This is 85 percent of the responses. Another 11 percent said it was at least "important." This means 99 percent of the grass-roots level workers believe literacy is important to the discipling process. Question 5 was a similar question worded slightly differently. "What level of importance does literacy play (the ability to read the Bible with understanding) in the maturing of the emerging church in India?" It is possible that the respondents did not understand the concept of discipleship clearly, so the term "maturing" was selected to assess if there was a discernable difference. There was not. They answered this question with an 89 percent "very important" response and 100 percent indicated literacy was at least "important" to the maturing of the emerging church in India.

---

215 India Census Data, 2001, http://www.censusindia.net/t_00_006.html.

Assumptions of the research community as to the importance of literacy in the discipleship process do not match the assessment of those involved in harvesting and discipleship. In the interview phase of this research, an attempt is made to measure behavioral differences related to discipleship that may indicate a correlation between literacy and discipleship. This is done later on in this section.

The final question on this survey seeks to determine the ability of the teachers/leaders in the emerging churches to read the Word of God with understanding. The following graph helps us understand the responses.

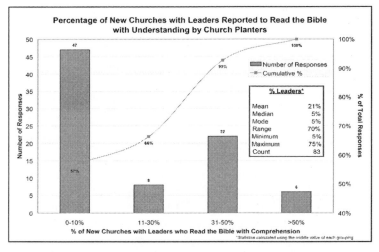

Table 8.4 Response to Survey Question 6 by Church Planters

This question revealed surprising results. First, both the middle value and the most frequent value is 5 percent. This is staggering! The teachers/leaders in the emerging church have similar literacy rates to the new believers. The average literacy rate is a meager 21 percent. Not only can very few of the new believers read the Bible, neither can their teachers. Of course, this was a preliminary review of a small sample of church planters in one state in India, but it is significant to the thesis of this book that literacy is a useful tool in the discipling of the emerging church in India. Certainly, at least for the leaders, it is more than useful, it is vital.

The first set of results from the grass-roots church planters indicated that the new believers in the emerging church in India are overwhelmingly illiterate with only a slightly higher percentage of the leaders able to read the Word of God for themselves. No matter what level of importance the reader may assign to literacy and discipleship, 85 percent of these church planters believe it is "very important" and 99 percent believe it is "important." These church planters believe that literacy is "useful" if not "critical" to the discipling of the emerging church in India.

An important question that the reader may ask concerns the ability of the participants in this survey to adequately make the assessment the questions require. Because this was unknown, it was useful to conduct a similar survey among church and ministry leaders to see if the results were similar. If there were wide discrepancies, one might indeed question the validity of the responses to survey 1. A comparison of the two is in the next section.

Survey 2–India Ministry Leaders

The initial survey conducted among 100 church planters in Andhra Pradesh was a precursor to conducting a similar survey among hundreds of different mission leaders from across India. Mission India held a Transformation Congress in Hyderabad in January of 2004 in which 1,500 ministry leaders from across India participated. One of the requirements for attendance was that all participants speak English. In gathering people from across a diverse country, it is necessary that there be a common spoken language because so many mother tongues are represented. During this four-day event, a survey on literacy in India was handed out to the delegates. The total responses handed in were 223. These represented opinions from 20 different states across India: Andhra Pradesh, Assam, Bihar, Chandigarh, Chhattisgarh, New Delhi, Gujarat, Haryana, Jammu and Kashmir, Jharkhand, Karnataka, Madhya Pradesh, Maharashtra, Manipur, Orissa, Tamil Nadu, Tripura, Uttaranchal, Uttar Pradesh, and West Bengal.

This grouping of ministry leaders represented a broad spectrum from across India both in terms of location and denominational affiliation. An important difference between this survey and the first one is that this was among ministry leaders versus church planters. There is also a significant educational level difference between the two groups. Ministry leaders had on average at least a college education versus an average of 10th grade for church planters. Ministry leaders will regularly travel outside their ministry area and meet with others involved in church planting efforts. However, it is the church planters who are most closely in touch with the new believers. It is through their witness that the emerging church is sprouting into existence. They are the ones visiting in their homes, praying with them, and shepherding these new flocks.

In this survey, adjustments were made to the survey question response options from survey 1. The selection was limited to four per question for questions 1–6. This was to simplify statistical analysis. Two open-ended questions were added to gather specific feedback from participants. The questions are both multiple-choice and open-ended. These are listed below:

2004 Nation Wide Literacy Survey
Consolidated Report
January 12-15, 2004

1. Of the new believers coming to Christ in the Churches and prayer cells you have planted, what percentage of them do you consider functionally literate?
    - ❏ 0 – 10% - **65**
    - ❏ 11% - 25% - **71**
    - ❏ 26% - 50% - **61**
    - ❏ Above 50% - **26**

    TOTAL =223

2. What percent of the believers in the new churches planted can read the Bible with understanding?
    - ❏ 0 – 10% - **76**
    - ❏ 11 – 25% - **83**
    - ❏ 26 – 50% - **48**
    - ❏ Above 50% - **15**

    TOTAL =222

3. In your opinion, what is the literacy rate among people coming to Christ across India?
    - ❏ 0 – 10% - **34**
    - ❏ 11% - 25% - **83**
    - ❏ 26% - 50% - **77**
    - ❏ Above 50% - **27**

    TOTAL=221

4. What level of importance does literacy Play (the ability to read the Bible with understanding) in the discipling of new believers ?
    - ❏ Very Important - **179**
    - ❏ Important - **37**
    - ❏ Somewhat Important - **02**
    - ❏ Unnecessary - **02**

    TOTAL=220

5. What percentage of the congregations in the Emerging Churches in your work have teachers/leaders that can read the Word of God with Understanding?
    - ❏ 0 – 10% - **51**
    - ❏ 11% - 25% - **65**
    - ❏ 26% - 50% - **69**
    - ❏ Above 50% - **37**

    TOTAL=222

6. How many Churches are in your Mission?
    - ❏ 0 – 10 - **93**
    - ❏ 11 – 25 - **53**
    - ❏ 26 – 50 - **14**
    - ❏ More than 50 - **55**

    TOTAL=215

Short Answer Questions:
7.   Do you feel it is important for new believers to read the Word of God? Why or why not?
8.   What is the biggest problem illiteracy creates for the church?

An analysis of each of the multiple-choice questions with graphs depicting the results follows. The open-ended questions were categorized and responses summarized.

Question 1: The ministry leaders at the Transformation Congress estimated the literacy rate of the new believers in the churches and prayer cells in their direct ministries as slightly higher than the church planters reporting in the earlier survey. The average literacy rate or mean sis 26 percent. The middle value estimates at 18 percent as well as the most frequent response. Please see Table 8.5 below.

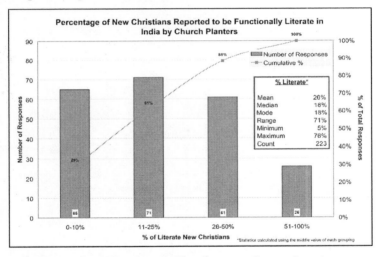

Table 8.5 Response to Question 1 by Transformation Congress Participants

The second question, which specifically identifies the literacy level of being able to read the Bible with comprehension, is slightly lower than question 1. The average drops from 26 percent to 22 percent and is highlighted in Table 8.6. This is consistent with the level of literacy required to read a book like the Bible. The Bible is not an easy book for a neo-literate to comprehend.

Similar to the responses submitted by the church planters in the initial survey, literacy in areas outside the respondents' sphere of influence assumes a higher understanding. The average is slightly higher from 26 percent to 30 percent just as the estimated rate in the first survey jumped from 8 percent in their ministry area to 14 percent in the rest of India.

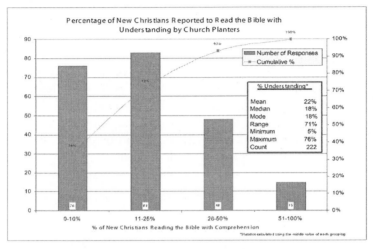

Table 8.6 Response to Question 2 by Transformation Congress Participants

What level of importance does literacy play (the ability to read the Bible with understanding) in the discipling of new believers? The church/ministry leaders have the same opinion as to the importance

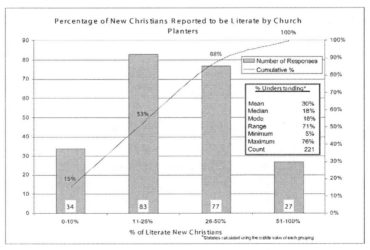

Table 8.7 Response to Question 3 by Transformation Congress Participants

of literacy in the discipling process. They overwhelmingly believe (81 percent) that literacy is "very important," and 98 percent believe it is "important" (see Table 8.8 below). There is no ambiguity in the minds of ministry leaders and church planters on the importance of literacy to spiritual growth. In questions 7 and 8, we will attempt to understand the thinking behind the answers to this question.

The answers to question 6 concerning the level of literacy among the teachers/leaders of the emerging church raises a grave concern for the sustainability of the rapid expansion of the emerging church in India. Historically, literate leaders did provide a critical vehicle for communicating truth to God's people, but can and do become corrupt when accountability does not exist. Accountability most often comes from those who can read the Word for themselves.

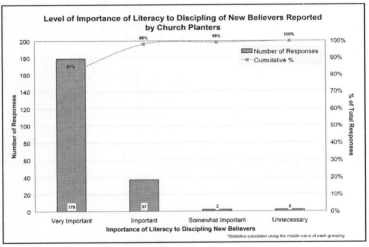

Table 8.8 Response to Question 4 by Transformation Congress Participants

According to this survey, over two-thirds of the leaders cannot read the Bible themselves (see Table 8.9). This presents a serious problem. Patience and focus are important in bringing literacy to the believers in the emerging church in India. Therefore, the title of this book is appropriate for this group. Urgency is required to bring literacy to church leaders.

In order to bring change, awareness of the problem is essential. Both surveys conducted for this book bring awareness of the inability of the leaders in the emerging church to disciple those under their care. When I started working on this book, I was unaware that the Word of God was a closed book to even the majority of the leaders.

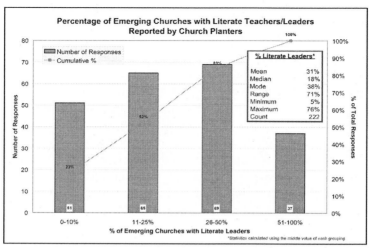

Table 8.9 Response to Question 5 by Transformation Congress Participants

This final objective question in the survey is to gain understanding of the ministry context of the respondents (see Table 8.10). There is a good mixture of small to larger ministries. This lends more credibility to the views expressed in this survey. If they were all to be from small ministries, one might assume that the perspective revealed in this research could be quite limited. One might reason that small ministries are confined to a very limited area and they have limited awareness of what is happening outside the district or state they live in. If all the data was from larger

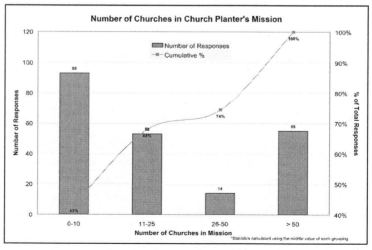

Table 8.10 Response to Question 6 by Transformation Congress Participants

ministries, one could assume that many of the leaders are not in touch with the ground realities of the emerging church in India. So often, larger ministry leaders have to become managers and fundraisers. This can result in them losing touch with field matters. The data below, along with the fact that this information included responses from 20 different states in India, gives the survey results a higher probability of reflecting the actual impact illiteracy has on the emerging church in India today.

The second section of this survey asked respondents to fill out open-ended questions. No suggestions were made for the responses. Respondents filled out the survey individually.

To better understand the responses, I established general summary categories. In the chart below (Table 8.11), the categories or main ideas are listed with the number of responses associated with that category. The categories are sorted by the number of responses. The total responses received were 247, as some respondents listed several different reasons why it is important for new believers to read the Word of God.

In order to understand the type of answers given, it is helpful to list under each category along with an answer or two given by the respondents. The answers are not edited. We must remember that the respondents all speak English as their second, third, or fourth language, but not as their mother tongue. In addition, answers were selected from different areas within India. The Indian State or Union Territory the respondent is from, as well as the church or mission, is noted.

S.No	Category Main Idea	No. of Persons
1	Reading is important to know and understand God's will	117
2	God's Word is the foundation for spiritual growth	30
3	Reading the Bible strengthens spiritual life	27
4	Sharing one's faith springs from knowledge of the truth	26
5	Just "Yes"; blank answers; and unrelated answers	24
6	Provides discernment of false teaching	6
7	Necessary for transformational discipleship	6
8	Releases a person from an unhealthy dependency on others	5
9	Reading the Bible gives light in darkness	3
10	Reading liberates the person	2
11	Literacy is not important	1

Table 8.11

Category 1: Reading is important to know and understand God's will
- "Important because God sounds very personal, familiar and more than anything revealing himself fully." Bihar, Gospel Echoing Missionary Society
- "Yes, it is very important for new believers to read the Word of God. Through which they come to know what is actually written in the Word of God. And they are able to use their free time in reading the Word of God." Uttaranchal, New Apostolic Church

Category 2: God's Word is the foundation for spiritual growth
- "The Bible is the Word of God. Without reading Bible we are incomplete." West Bengal, Northern Evangelical Lutheran Church

Category 3: Reading the Bible strengthens spiritual life
- "Yes, to make strong believers and leaders." Maharashtra, Indian Friends Fellowship Church
- "Because the Word of God is the only spiritual food which can satisfy our spiritual hunger." West Bengal, D.E.W.T Ministries

Category 4: Sharing one's faith springs from knowledge of the truth
- "Yes it is very important to new believers who can read the Bible. At least if they can read I believe they can teach another people and then revolution can come to their tribes and Dalit people of Madhya Pradesh." Madhya Pradesh, Evangelical Lutheran Church in Madhya Pradesh

Category 5: Just "Yes"; blank answers; and unrelated answers
- There were twelve who just answered "yes" with no explanation, six who left this question blank, and four others whose answers were not understandable.

Category 6: Provides discernment of false teaching
- "Yes, because they will not be misled by others false teaching." Assam, Chinai Chuk Baptist Church
- "It will help them to know what God wants us to do otherwise they will not know which one is God's spirit and which is the devil's spirit." Andhra Pradesh, Mennonite Brethren Church

Category 7: Necessary for transformational discipleship
- "I believe that transformation of life, spiritually, economically, socially. I believe Bible can bring changes so that reading and understanding of Word of God is important." Karnataka, Agape Educational Society

Category 8: Releases a person from an unhealthy dependency on others
- "For the new believers it is very important to read the Word of God. Because without reading they can not very good in understanding the Word of God and always they have to depend on others. So, they should be literate." Orissa, Assembly of Indian Christians

Category 9: Reading the Bible gives light in darkness
- "Unless one reads the Word of God, he is in darkness and do not know where he is walking. God's Word is a lamp to the feet and light for path Ps.119:105." Andhra Pradesh, Hebron Mission India

Category 10: Reading liberates the person
- "The verses of the Bible can follow the new believers when they are oppresses in their daily life." Apostolic Prayer House

Category 11: Literacy is not important
- Only one response out of 230 surveys handed in said reading the Bible was not important for new believers.

The overwhelming opinion of the respondents to question 7 is that reading the Bible is important for new believers. This is for a variety of reasons: from knowledge, to spiritual growth, to strengthening one's faith, to witnessing, to holistic development, to move from unhealthy spiritual dependency and finally to avoiding the snare of the cults.

The final question in this survey is an attempt to determine what effects illiteracy has on the church. The question read, "What is the biggest problem illiteracy creates for the church?" The following chart categorizes the responses to this question. The answers are presented according to a general category as with question 7, so the reader can listen to Indian church leaders as they relate the effects of illiteracy on their churches.

S.No	Main Idea	No. of Persons
1	Illiteracy hinders church and personal growth	55
2	Back sliding & poor in the spiritual life	54
3	Irrelevant Answers; Blank Answers	38
4	Social problems	23
5	Misunderstanding God's Word	21
6	Difficult to communicate with	15
7	Dependence on others	7
8	Illiterates cannot become leaders	6
9	Illiteracy is not a problem	3

Table 8.12

Category 1: Illiteracy hinders church and personal growth
- "(1) Most of the people are busy with their own work (2) Churches are not aware of the literacy of the church people (3) There is no systematic study/book for the church people (4) Church is totally sleeping regarding the church people illiteracy." West Bengal, Church of the Nazarene
- "The biggest problem illiteracy creates for the church is chaos and confusion among the church community." Manipur, InTouch
- "Illiteracy hinders believers in understanding the Word of God thus their growth in the Word becomes slack. The church suffers to become a reproducing multiplying church." Orissa, Orissa Follow-up

Category 2: Backsliding and poor in spiritual life
- "Illiteracy creates big harm for the church. Illiterates believe rumours immediately. If they know the literacy, they never believe rumours against God. Illiterates left the God by not experiencing and understanding. They can hear only but not read so they can't understand the Word of God." Andhra Pradesh, Integrated Rural Development Service Society
- "We have to carry everyday, otherwise they will go down." Jammu and Kashmir, Bethel Gospel Church
- "Economic—Poverty, Socially—Backwardness, Spiritually—Darkness." Andhra Pradesh, Arakuvalley Mission

Category 3: Irrelevant answers; blank answers
- It is important to note that this question had more in this category than question 7. A reason for this might be that the question required a different level of thinking. There were 10 answers that were blank. More appeared confused by this with 28 answers fitting into this section of this category alone.

Category 4: Social problems
- "(1) Superstitious (2) Witchcraft (3) Blind beliefs (4) Don't have position (5) Cannot do mission work (6) Don't attend important occasions." Karnataka, Indian Evangelical Lutheran Church
- "Religion and Caste problem, language problem." Tamil Nadu, India Evangelical Lutheran Church

Category 5: Misunderstanding God's Word
- "The biggest problem illiteracy creates is misunderstanding." Andhra Pradesh, Jesus Prayer House Ministries
- "They will create wrong statements about God and the Bible and the church. And some of them become totally against the Kingdom of God." Andhra Pradesh, Baptist Church

Category 6: Difficult to communicate with
- "The biggest problem of illiteracy creates for the church is the communication hindrance of the Gospel making disciples." Jharkhand, Assemblies of God Church
- "Illiterate cannot understand the Word of God as a literate can understand. He hears only and forgets soon but literate reads and remembers. Illiteracy is like a blindness day time." Bihar, Prem Dham

Category 7: Dependence on others
- "Depending only other church people, so it creates biggest problem." Assam, Adibari Baptist Church

Category 8: Illiterates cannot become leaders
- "Biggest problem is they cannot read the Bible. They cannot read the songs from the hymn books. They cannot be leaders and pastors." West Bengal, Northern Evangelical Lutheran Church

According to these leaders, illiteracy has a crippling effect on the emerging church in India today. One might ask whether or not the ill effects of illiteracy are also conditions of churches whose members are all literate. Literate churches are often stagnant, do not reproduce, are often filled with rumors and misunderstandings. However, they generally are not economically poor, socially backward and spiritually blind. They do not live with superstition, witchcraft, and blind beliefs. They do not live with *"blindness day time"* (see response to question 8 above from the State of Bihar). They do not live with illiterate leaders who are incapable of teaching the Word of God because they cannot read it. They do not generally live with teachers who thus distort the truth because they know no better.

The purpose of this book was not to compare illiterate emerging churches with literate mainline congregations within India. The comparison sought is between literate and nonliterate believers in the emerging churches. The final section of the research portion of this book attempts to discern differences in measurable behaviors associated with discipleship between literate and nonliterate believers in the emerging church.

One other comment is important to make before proceeding to the next section. It was noted after the discussion on the first survey that the ability of the participants to make an appropriate assessment to the questions is an important consideration. However, since the responses to both the first survey given by minimally educated church planters and the responses from the second group of theologically educated leaders were consistent, I believe the respondents understood and answered the questions properly.

Phase 2 – Impact of Literacy on Spiritual Maturity

The purpose of this final survey was to assess literacy's measurable impact on believers in the emerging church in India. The first challenge is wrestling with whether or not discipleship is actually measurable. In the Western church, there is hesitancy in establishing specific targets in ministry efforts. Very few churches set "Great Commission" goals. Concrete targets, if any, are limited to attendance and budget. Few Western churches place measurable goals before their congregation. For example, you would seldom, if ever, see a specific goal that in the next year the church is praying that God would allow them to bring 500 new believers in the kingdom and start 10 new churches. Unlike India, not many would dare to paint these goals on the front of the worship center next to the pulpit like a huge billboard and publish them in the bulletin each week. Public pronouncements of clear objectives are seldom made because of the accountability associated with it.

Measurement is more often than not avoided at the local church and denominational level. This is partly because it is difficult to define specific measures of a church's health. It is reasoned that spiritual growth cannot be, or perhaps should not be, measured. But it need not be this way. Many churches in India today are unafraid of accountability. One of Mission India's partners in Tamil Nadu, Peace Blessing Church, has the church's goals painted on the walls next to the pulpit. This is where many churches post the song numbers for the day. Every week the entire church body is reminded of why they come together. It is not just for worship and Bible teaching, but also for blessing others. They actually look ahead to what they are going to do together and look back on what God has done through them.

Is it possible to set measurable objectives for personal spiritual growth? Is it wise to attempt to determine if a person is actually growing as a disciple of Jesus Christ? Is it even possible to measure something spiritual? Should it be attempted? In the Sermon on the Mount, Jesus concludes with the importance of building on a solid foundation. He says, "Anyone who listens to my teaching and obeys me is wise, like a person who builds a house on solid rock" (Matthew 7:24). James says, "And remember, it is a message to obey, not just to listen to. If you don't obey, you are only fooling yourself" (James 1:22). From these passages, it appears that the Scriptures teach that obedience is concrete and measurable. This matter is of such importance that it is part of the Great Commission and evidence of discipleship. "Teach these new disciples to obey all the commands I have given you" (Matthew 28:20). But should an attempt be made to measure discipleship?

This is actually a critical question of this book. Is literacy useful to the discipling of the emerging church in India? If it is presumptuous or potentially dangerous to measure growth in discipleship, then this whole effort is perhaps in vain. Spiritual growth can remain in the subjective realm. However, not challenging this mindset can leave the church in a weak and potentially hazardous position. As Jesus says, "The decisive issue is whether they obey my Father in heaven" (Matthew 7:21).

Historical information on literacy and discipleship is limited. The majority of the church was illiterate the first fifteen centuries. This was not the case with the leaders. The emerging church in India today is basically illiterate, including the leaders. Most would agree that literacy is useful if not critical for those responsible for shepherding the flock of

God. But does it really make any difference in the life of the individual believer? If so, what would those differences look like and do they have anything to do with discipleship?

However, there are reasonable fears in measurement. Perhaps the benchmarks established will have little to do with true spirituality. Perhaps, in the process of measurement, the result will be another contribution to the long list of legalisms the church has created and lived with since its earliest days. And so often, these benchmarks contribute nothing to discipleship but only uphold tradition and a false sense of spirituality.

A risk is taken here. The potential downside is adding another brand of legalism in attempting to measure discipleship. But spiritual growth should be able to be measurably discerned. Therefore, a decision was made to sit with several staff members of our sister organization in India, and discuss the possibility of constructing a questionnaire that could give insight into the usefulness of literacy in discipleship.

This is different from the first two surveys already reported on in this chapter. First, it was helpful to determine the views of the leaders of the emerging church. Unquestionably, they believe literacy makes an important contribution to discipleship. With this next survey, a measurement tool was constructed to assess quantitative and qualitative differences between illiterate and literate followers of Jesus Christ. A copy of the questions along with the tabulated responses is found in Appendix 3.

Selection of Control Groups
In order to make a measurement assessment, two communities were selected: one entirely rural and the other, living within an urban area, though in a slum. Both groups are from the state of Andhra Pradesh. In each group, a total of 50 respondents were selected. All claimed to be followers of Jesus Christ. Twenty-five of the respondents were literate and the other 25 nonliterate. This is the case for both the rural and urban control groups. Therefore, a total of 100 respondents were interviewed, half literate and half nonliterate. This survey is called a 2x2 factorial design with two variables (urban and rural) with two levels of each variable (literate versus nonliterate).

Description of Control Groups
Rural group—Khammam District
In most areas in India, a people group does not live isolated from other people groups. Most communities include several different people groups. This is the case with the literacy work conducted by V. David

on the border of Andhra Pradesh and Chhattisgarh. The people groups included in this survey are Konda Reddis and the Koyas. The term Konda Reddi derived "from the words konda (hill) and redid (headman)."[216] These people live on top of the hills in the Khammam district in Andhra Pradesh. According to David, they say, "We are living on top of the hills because we are the top people of the Koyas." From a caste perspective, their literal elevated living position also results in the position they hold in that community. They are a predominantly rural community, with "98.94 percent of their population inhabiting rural areas."[217] "Marriage by service, capture, negotiation, courtship, elopement and exchange are common. . . . A Konda Reddi man carries simple implements such as a small knife, and a bow and arrow. . . . Sickness and disease are attributed to the wrath of malevolent deities or angry spirits. . . . The 1981 census records 99.39 percent of the Konda Reddi as followers of Hinduism, 0.44 percent as Christian and 0.17 percent as those who have not stated their religion."[218] David reports a high incidence of alcoholism, but because of their worship of the hill goddesses, they cannot make the liquor in their homes. The 1981 census reports the literacy rate "at 7.77 percent."[219]

Like the Konda Reddi, the Koyas are also from the hill areas and Koya is from the same root word as "Konda meaning hill."[220] Their main food is Javvari or tapioca. "They are experts in indigenous medicine and go around selling it."[221] With any sickness they consult the witch doctor and use the herbal medicines they produce. Alcoholism is also a serious problem with the Koyas. "They profess local forms of Hinduism and have family and village deities. The 1981 census records 99.89 percent of the Koya as followers of Hinduism, 0.04 percent as Christian, 0.02 percent as Muslims and 0.05 percent as those who have not stated their religion. . . . Their literacy rate according to the 1981 census is only 7.89 percent."[222] David reports the illiteracy rate at 99 percent in the specific area he is working in. Because of this, "a large section of them are indebted to moneylenders and shopkeepers."[223]

---

216 K. S. Singh, *The Scheduled Tribes,* People of India National Series, Volume III (New Delhi: Oxford University Press, 1994), 587.
217 Ibid.
218 Ibid., 588.
219 Ibid., 589.
220 Ibid., 632.
221 Ibid., 633.
222 Ibid.
223 Ibid.

Urban group—Rangareddy District

Banjaras are traditionally a nomadic community. During British colonial rule, these Gypsy nomads of India were given the name Banjara. An estimated 20 million Banjaras inhabit India today. They live in "groups called tandas, each comprising six to twenty families. The doctrine of collective responsibility operates among the members of the tanda."[224] Most Banjaras live in thatched huts with single rooms, regardless of the family size. This one room is used for cooking, eating, and sleeping. They are categorized mainly as Hindus, though traditionally they are animists. The Hindu population is "99.87 percent in 1981."[225] The literacy rate during the same year was listed at 16.94 percent.[226]

Hyderabad is home to many Banjaras. In fact, a major section of the new city is named "Banjara Hills" because of its former occupants. It is now one of the posh sections of this large metropolitan area. The Banjaras themselves are relegated to the slums in and around the city of Hyderabad. The area where this survey was conducted is in the city slums of Hyderabad.

Theory Behind Construction of Interview Questions

An attempt was made in the construction of the interview questions to assess both qualitative and quantitative indicators of spiritual growth. The categories chosen were knowledge, experience, ability, and behavior. The intent of the questions was to determine whether or not literacy made a discernible difference in discipleship in the lives of the believers in both a rural and urban setting.

The methodology in gathering this information was through personal interview. Since one half of the respondents were illiterate, it was impossible for them to read and fill out the answers to a survey. Because of this, it was also necessary to interview the literates so the process would be consistent. A total of three interviewers were used in the process of gathering this information.

Summary of Findings

Personal Information—The average age in the four groups varied from 27 to 38. There were a total of 55 females interviewed and 45 males. In each of the nonliterate groups, there were 16 females and 9 males. This is

---

224   K. S. Singh, *India's Communities, A–G*, People of India National Series, Vol. IV (New Delhi: Oxford University Press, 1998), 269.

225   Singh, *The Scheduled Tribes*, 89.

226   Ibid.

consistent with the overall difference in literacy rates in India from male to female. According to the 2001 census the spread between the sexes in terms of literacy is 19.9 percent in the state of Andhra Pradesh. Among the Banjara's "the census returns 30.37 percent of the males and 4.27 percent of the females as literate."[227] A table of the summary of the results of the interviews is found in Appendix 3.

Knowledge—According to the answers given, a clear difference in knowledge of who Jesus was is not apparent. Among illiterates in the rural setting, 12 stated that Jesus was the healer. Only three of the literates responded in a similar manner. There appears to be a stronger emphasis on the miraculous among illiterates. However, in the urban setting this distinction was not present.

Experience—A clear difference in this category also does not appear to exist, except in the area of healing. In the answer to question 2, "Why did you accept Jesus into your life?" nonliterates responded 17 times that healing was the key, whereas literates responded nine times. This can be an indicator that experience has more weight with an illiterate than the revealed Word. The second most frequent response by church and ministry leaders to the question, "What is the biggest problem illiteracy creates for the church?" was that it resulted in backsliding and a poor spiritual life. An experienced-based faith can be more susceptible to backsliding, especially when significant miracles do not recur.

Ability—There are obvious differences in this category. All of the literates in both groups said they can read the Bible and read it at least weekly. Most literates state they read the Bible daily (33 out of 50). Even though the illiterates cannot read the Bible, 32 value it enough to have one in their home. At the same time, 27 of the illiterates had no idea why the Bible was important. The most frequent response was that it was a "holy book" (12 responses). In contrast to the poor understanding of the importance of the Bible, the majority of literates saw it as a practical guide for spiritual growth and direction. This is a critical distinction. When the church and ministry leaders in the second survey were asked, "Do you feel it is important for new believers to read the Word of God? Why or why not?" their number one response by an overwhelming margin (117 responses) was "reading is important to know and understand God's will." The next closest response was mentioned by 30 people. Based on the answers given by the illiterate

---

227   Ibid., 89.

Christian community in this survey, it is reasonable to conclude that discernment of God's will is stunted by illiteracy. This conclusion is consistent with the broad observations of Indian Christian ministry leaders. The implications of this distinction are fleshed out even more clearly in the behavior section of this survey.

Behavior—There are significant noticeable differences in the behaviors reported by the survey respondents in this category. The only question where the answers appear similar is relating to prayer. Both groups in both areas all reported a consistent prayer life. This is not unexpected as Hinduism is also a religion of prayer. People converting from Hinduism would easily transition into a regular prayer life after following Christ. The questions where the differences were noticeable are:

1. Leading people to Christ—The difference between literates and nonliterates is very noticeable in the answers to this question. The observable differences are that the nonliterate on average has led .9 people to Christ, with the middle value for the 50 respondents at "0." For those who could read the Bible, the average number of people they led to Christ was 4.8 with the middle value at 3. On average, there is a five-fold increase. Even when we isolate the urban area, average value is 3.5, or nearly 4 times the illiterate average. Again the observations made by the ministry leaders in survey number 2, as to the biggest problem illiteracy creates for the church, confirms this data. Their number one response was that it hinders church and personal growth. According to the data given by both literate and illiterate believers in both an urban and rural setting, literacy has an important relationship to the fulfillment of the Great Commission.

2. Prayer—There is little distinguishable difference in the stated prayer life between the literate and illiterate believers.

3. Hospitality—In the urban setting, one half of the illiterate group did not answer this question while only five of the literates did not indicate any type of hospitality shown. In the rural group, eight of the illiterates said they seldom show hospitality with the balance signifying no hospitality at all. Fourteen of the literate believers in the rural area showed they are hospitable frequently, nine said sometimes or seldom, and only two said they did not invite people into their home. The difference in hospitality between the literate and illiterate groups points to

the literates' broader understanding of biblical relationships.

4. Forgiveness—This is a difficult quality to measure, though an attempt is made by posing the question, "How do you respond when somebody hurts you?" The illiterates indicate they fight and quarrel more than the literates, 15 responses to 5, or a 3 to 1 ratio. Second, the literates reveal they forgive, pray, or respond in love for the person at a ratio of 24 to 7. This may show that the literate believers again have a broader understanding of the biblical teaching on revenge and seek to implement it.

5. Compassion—The way a believer responds to a person in need also can signify the level of spiritual maturity. The Scriptures consistently teach that followers of Jesus should be generous. Again, the literates in this survey indicate that they help more people on average than the non-literate. The ratio is nearly 4 to 1. Literates also were able to specify the type of help given much more clearly and more often than the non-literates. Literates appear more obedient in the area of compassion than the illiterates.

6. Finance—This category, along with witnessing, reveal some of the largest contrasts between literate and illiterate believers. In the urban area, the literate believers earned more than double the income than the illiterates. The contrast is not so great in the rural area, partly because there are less income generating opportunities and partly because many of the literate survey participants did not have a job where they actually generated cash income. Nonetheless, the literate group earned 11 percent more than the illiterates even in the rural jungle area. What is most striking, however, is the significant difference in giving. Not only did the amount increase, but the percentage of total income increased. In terms of discipleship, we find more obedience in the area of finance with the literate group.

Implications

In almost every question posed to the literate and illiterate believers in both the urban and rural settings, the answers reveal that literates not only have a greater understanding of biblical obedience, but a greater obedience. There was little difference between the rural and urban groups. The information gathered needs to be tested in a broader context but clearly reflects the usefulness of literacy in the discipling process of the emerging church in India.

The results of all three of the surveys are consistent with one another. The first two express opinions of the leaders of the emerging church in India as to the level of illiteracy in the church and the importance of literacy. The final survey, conducted to investigate the validity of the thesis topic by questioning the membership in the emerging church, revealed findings consistent with the views of the leaders expressed in the first two surveys. Literacy is important in the discipling process. It not only aids the believer in knowing and understanding God's will, it strengthens him or her in their walk of obedience in the area of witness, hospitality, forgiveness, compassion and finance.

Chapter 9
Implementing Literacy as a Discipling Strategy

Discipleship in the emerging church in India is hindered by illiteracy. In a positive sense, literacy is a useful tool in the discipling of the emerging church in India. The church is growing rapidly among the poor, oppressed communities in India. Most of these people are illiterate.

Church and mission leaders across India have established a target of 20 percent of the Indian population being Christian by the year 2020. This is a net increase of 1,000 percent in little more than a decade. The literacy rate in the emerging church currently is low even among leadership. With the type of growth proposed, the lack of ability to read the Word of God will have crippling results on the sustainability of these new believers.

Much of current missions focus emphasizes the importance of placing the Word of God in the hands of people. According to David B. Barrett in the *World Christian Encyclopedia,* the Scripture placement goals for India have been surpassed.[228] Even according to the research conducted for this book, 60 percent of the nonliterates had Bibles in their homes they could not read. The written Word only brings value if one can read it. It would seem that a shift in strategy is advisable from Scripture placement to teaching leaders and believers to read the Word of God they already have in their hands. Unfortunately, it is easier to raise money for Bibles whether or not they are needed, than to teach people to read the Bible. It is important that our fundraising reflect genuine ministry needs and not drive ministry strategy. The easiest way to raise money may not actually contribute to the completion of the Great Commission.

Insights
Oral teaching methods can help accelerate world evangelization. However, an illiterate believer remains spiritually and developmentally

---

228   David B. Barrett, *World Christian Encyclopedia*, Volume 1 (New York: Oxford University Press, 2001), 857.

stunted, wobbly in standing on his own, unable to shed the chains of poverty and oppression, and ultimately in a very precarious position to remain grounded in truth. Literacy is useful and strategic in the task of evangelism and discipleship. Many communities closed to traditional evangelism are open to learning to read. This is even true when the teaching tools are biblically based. Literacy is also useful in the discipling process. It equips the believer to read the Bible with a greater potential of spiritual growth. This is evident from the research done among literate and illiterate believers for this book. In addition to spiritual obedience, changes in life expectancy, knowledge, and living standards are also significantly improved with literacy. This is demonstrated in Table 7.4 where the measurable income increase as a result of literacy is 57 percent. This moves a person from 23 percent below the absolute poverty line to 22 percent above it.

Previous research on the relationship of literacy and discipleship is quite limited. The critical importance of this matter was elevated by the working group entitled "Making Disciples of Oral Learners" at the Lausanne Conference in 2004. The significance of the research done by this conference to this book is the recognition that "1.5 billion people in the world have never been introduced to reading and writing" and "at least 67 percent of the world's people are either non-literate or functionally illiterate."[229] As a nation, India comprises the largest percentage of nonliterates. Oral learners, according to this working group, do not respond to traditional literate teaching methodologies. Although I agree with this premise, the ability to read the written page is not peripheral in the discipling process. A holistic approach to discipleship needs to recognize and address the devastating consequences of illiteracy on all aspects of life. Discipleship is a transformational process on the whole person.

There has been a great deal of research done on the relationship of literacy to development. The contribution of this book to this body of research is limited. However, there is a clear connection between literacy and Christian social responsibility. John R.W. Stott talks about our neighbor as "a body-soul-in-community."[230] The point is that we are not just bodiless souls that must be evangelized or just soulless bodies that must be cared for. We are image bearers of

---

229   *Fast Facts: On Orality, Literacy and Chronological Bible Storying*, http://www.chrono-logicalbiblestorying.com/articles/fast_facts.htm.

230   John R.W. Stott, *Christian Mission in the Modern World* (Downers Grove, IL: Inter-Varsity Press, 1975), 30.

the divine living in community. Literacy proved to be a critical tool leading up to the Reformation. Through this study we found important differences between literate and nonliterate communities in India today. Greater compassion, forgiveness, hospitality, self-discipline, and financial independence resides among literate believers in the emerging churches.

Where do we go from here?

Although this is just one study and does not reflect a complete understanding of the literacy level of the emerging church in India today, there are a number of important implications that must be considered.

Awareness—Prior to writing this book, I was aware of the crippling effects of literacy upon a person and the limitations it places on discipleship. In addition, I was unaware of the alarming low literacy level of the leadership in the emerging church in India. Church and mission leaders within India need to become aware of the unstable nature of the emerging church due to the inability of new believers and leaders to read the Word of God for themselves.

Awareness also needs to alert leaders of the unproven assumption that the nonliterate has a greater memory capacity than the literate. This leaves the church in India wide open for heretical assaults, and a reversion back to Hinduism and syncretism.

Strategy—Missionaries in India will do well to carry a Bible in one hand and a literacy primer in the other. Literacy opens the door to communities who are closed to traditional evangelistic techniques. It is also useful in discipling the majority of new believers in the emerging church. Literacy is also critical for those in leadership. Churches led by illiterate but zealous men and women will be much more subject to syncretism. One of the main goals of all Great Commission ministries should be that the leaders of the new churches are able to read the Word of God. They can only lead with the authority of the Scriptures if they have access to them.

Holistic ministry—Discipleship is a transformational process and is not limited to the spiritual dimension of life. Literacy is an effective tool in transformational discipleship. Along with strengthening spiritual development as demonstrated in the research for this book, it is a critical contributor to human development. Literacy has long been linked to increased longevity, knowledge, and decent living standards. Giving someone the gift of literacy is a tangible act of obedience to Jesus' call to love your neighbor as yourself. A literacy program is an excellent way for ministries to be a part of fulfilling the Great Compassion.

Written languages—Literate believers demonstrated greater levels of obedience according to the research conducted. An awareness of these findings can be a great benefit to those committed to discipling the nations, especially in areas where there are large concentrations of unreached peoples. This does not solve the problem that exists where spoken languages are yet to be put in writing. Yet this does not present as big a problem as one might first imagine. In most areas where a tribal language may be the mother tongue, they speak a state or official language as well. The diversity of languages in India today presents unique challenges to even indigenous missionaries. However, literacy can be available today to most peoples. According to 1991 census data, 96.3 percent of all Indians speak scheduled languages that are all written.[231] Orality will continue to be the primary tool where written language is not available.

Leadership development — Illiterate leaders pose a serious threat for the stability of the emerging church. Emerging church growth is often occurring through the formation of house churches. The size of each congregation is small, based on the limitations of the meeting places. Because of this, the need for a great number of literate leaders is significant. A concerted effort to bring literacy to emerging church leaders must become a priority in our mission efforts.

Primacy of Scripture—The Word of God is the foundation of faith in the one living and true God. We come to know Him through the pages of this precious volume. Unfortunately, the Bible is a closed book to the illiterate unless he or she has the opportunity to hear it read. In India today, two-thirds of the emerging churches do not even have this option. An illiterate leadership cannot read the Word of God to an illiterate membership. Martin Luther wanted the German people to be able to read the Bible in simple German as a mother would speak to her child. The translation of the Scriptures into German, along with the availability of the printing press, brought about a reformation transforming Christendom and Western civilization. Without literacy, the temptation of the powerful to control and oppress will repeat itself. It is not enough

---

231   *Central Institute of Indian Languages*, http://www.ciil.org/languages/indian.html.

to distribute Bibles. People must be able to read them.

The unbelieving community in India is open to literacy, for it brings them tangible value they can immediately feel: no more exploitation, no more cheating, healthier lives, educated children. And the emerging church in India is in great need of being able to read God's Word for themselves. It has transforming power. It has the power to *BLESS* the nation of India:

> It benefits the...
> *B*ody through better health awareness
> *L*abor through allowing the learning of better skills
> *E*motions through understanding the tremendous value God
> gives every human created in His Image
> *S*ocial life by elevating the individual and community and
> *S*piritual life through God's transforming love.

Timothy Beals, in an article in the *Faith and Action Study Bible*, says, "The ability to read and write is no less central to the understanding of God's Good News"[232] today as it was for Daniel. He continues with a statement, which is the essence of discipleship: "Reading and writing open the door to knowing and doing."[233]

John records in his Gospel: "Jesus' disciples saw him do many other miraculous signs besides the ones recorded in this book. But these are written so that you may believe that Jesus is the Messiah, the Son of God, and that by believing in him you will have life" (John 20:30-31). These words are written so others may read, know, and pass on the truth. Without the ability to read, we leave the emerging church crippled. And our task of completing the Great Commission will remain undone.

---

232 *Faith in Action Study Bible* (Grand Rapids: Zondervan, 2005), 1390.
233 Ibid.

Appendix 1
Literacy and Discipleship Survey

Literacy and Discipleship Survey
   Name:

   Age:

   Sex:

   Location:

   Community:

   Interviewer's Name:

   Date:

   Literate Or Nonliterate:

Knowledge
   1.   Who is Jesus?

   2.   What did He do?

Experience:
   1.   What was your life like before accepting Jesus?

   2.   Why did you accept Jesus into your life?

   3.   What changes have taken place in your life since accepting Jesus?

Ability:

1. Can you read the Bible? Yes/No

2. How often do you read the Bible? Daily, Twice Weekly, Weekly, Monthly, Never

3. Do you have a Bible in your home? Yes/No

4. Why is the Bible important?

Behavior:

1. How many people have you led to Christ?

2. What are your prayer timings?

3. How often do you invite people into your home?

4. How do you respond when somebody hurts you?

5. How many people in need have you helped?
   What type of help have you offered?

6. What is your daily income?
   How much do you give to the church each week?

7. If the interviewee identified specific behavioral problems before accepting Christ and they are listed below, please have them respond:

   • Do you still commit adultery? Yes/No   If so, how often?
   • Do you still fight? Yes/No   If so, how often?
   • Do you still get drunk? Yes/No   If so, how often?

Appendix 2
Literacy Survey

10 Institute of Community Transformation Schools in Andhra Pradesh Who Have Attended the ICT Alumni Conference in October 2003

1. Of the new believers coming to Christ in the Churches and prayer cells you have planted, what percentage of them do you consider functionally literate?
    - ❏ 0 – 5% - **41**
    - ❏ 5% - 10% - **15**
    - ❏ 10% - 20% - **13**
    - ❏ 20% - 30% - **11**
    - ❏ 30% - 40% - **02**
    - ❏ 40% - 50%
    - ❏ Above 50%

2. What percent of the believers in the new churches planted can read the Bible with understanding?
    - ❏ 0 – 5% - **46**
    - ❏ 5 – 10% - **21**
    - ❏ 10 – 20% - **03**
    - ❏ 20 – 30% - **11**
    - ❏ 30 – 40% - **01**
    - ❏ 40 – 50%
    - ❏ Above 50%

3. In your opinion, what is the literacy rate among people coming to Christ across India?
    - ❏ 0 – 5% - **18**
    - ❏ 5 – 10% - **34**
    - ❏ 10 – 20% - **07**
    - ❏ 20 – 30% - **13**
    - ❏ 30 – 40% - **10**
    - ❏ 40 – 50% - **01**
    - ❏ Above 50%

4. What level of importance does literacy Play (the ability to read the Bible with understanding) in the discipling of new believers ?
    - ❏ Very Important - **71**
    - ❏ Important - **11**
    - ❏ Somewhat Important - **01**
    - ❏ Unnecessary

5. What level of importance does literacy play (the ability to read the Bible with understanding) in the maturing of the emerging Church in India ?
    - ❏   Very Important - **74**
    - ❏   Important - **09**
    - ❏   Somewhat Important
    - ❏   Unnecessary

6. What percentage of the congregations in the Emerging Churches in your work have teachers/leaders that can read the Word of God with Understanding?

    - ❏   0 – 5% - **31**
    - ❏   5 – 10% - **16**
    - ❏   10 – 20% - **06**
    - ❏   20 – 30% - **02**
    - ❏   30 – 40% - **19**
    - ❏   40 – 50% - **03**
    - ❏   50 – 75% - **05**
    - ❏   75 – 100% - **01**

Name:_____

Church/Mission/
Organization:_____

State:_____**Dist:**_____

Date:_____

Appendix 3
Urban Area Survey Snapshot

Literates

Sex	Persons
Male	15
Female	10

Age Range	25-45
Average Age	37

Knowledge

1. Who is Jesus?	
Answer Provided	**Responses**
Lord	9
Savior, God	6
God	5
no answer	5

Ability

3. Do they have Bible?	
Yes	25
No	0

4. Why is the Bible important?	
Answer Provided	**Responses**
Good & Great Book	6
God speaks & book of life	5
It guides	5
Holy Book	4
Encouraging	4
Jesus life story	1

Experience

1. What was their life before accepting Christ?	
Answer Provided	**Responses**
Drunkard, smoking & dancing, fighting	12
Worldly life	8
Adultery	4
No peace	1

2. Why did they accept Jesus in to their life?	
Answer Provided	**Responses**
To get peace	8
To change life	6
To get salavation	5
Healing	3
Wife's prayer	2
Some one said	1

3. What changes have taken place after accepting Christ?	
Answer Provided	**Responses**
Left old bad habits	15
Got peace	6
Got Salvation	3
Family saved	1

Behavior

1. How many people have they led to Christ?

Average	Responses
1-2	11
3-4	6
above 5	7
No reply	1
Average	3.5

4. How do they respond when they were Hurt?

Answer Provided	Responses
Keep quiet	17
Fight Back	3
Praying for them	3
Quarrelling	1
No answer	1

5. How many people in need have they helped?

Average	1.8

5b. What type of help have you offered?

Answer Provided	Responses
Need based help	12
No answer	9
Giving advice	2
Giving rice	2

6. What is their Daily Income

Income (Rs.)	No. of People
0 - 50	3
51 - 100	11
101 - 150	8
Housewives	3
Average Income	Rs. 87

6b. How much do they give to the church?

Range	No. of People
1 - 5	8
5 - 10	15
11 & above	2
Average weekly contribution	7

7c. Do they still fight?

Yes	4

Urban Area Survey Snapshot

Non-Literates

Sex	Persons
Male	9
Female	16

Age Range	28-49
Average Age	38

Knowledge

1. Who is Jesus?

Answer Provided	Responses
God	14
Lord	5
no answer	5
Savior, God	1

Ability

3. Do they have Bible?

Yes	13
No	12

4. Why is the Bible important?

Answer Provided	Responses
Holy Book	12
No answer	10
Good Book	2
Protects	1
Encouraging	0
God speaks & book of life	0
It guides	0

Experience

1. What was their life before accepting Christ?

Answer Provided	Responses
Drunkard, smoking & dancing, fighting	17
Worldly life	5
Idol worshippers	2
Adultery	1

2. Why did they accept Jesus in to their life?

Answer Provided	Responses
Healing	7
Someone said	6
Saviour	5
To get peace	5
Expecting Miracle	1
To change life	1

3. What changes have taken place after accepting Christ?

Answer Provided	Responses
Left Old bad habits	8
Got peace	8
Happy life & Fear of God	3
Family Saved	3
Miracle Happened	3

Behavior		

1. How many people have they led to Christ?

Average	Responses
1-2	13
3-4	0
above 5	0
No reply	12
Average	0.96

6. What is their Daily Income

Income (Rs.)	No. of People
0 - 50	18
51 - 100	2
101 - 150	0
Housewives	5
Average Income	Rs. 38

4. How do they respond when they were Hurt?

Answer Provided	Responses
Keep quiet	7
Fight Back	5
Quarrelling	4
Leaving the place	4
No answer	4
Compromise	1

6b. How much do they give to the church?

Range	No. of People
1 - 5	24
5 - 10	0
11 & above	0
Average weekly contribution	2.4

5. How many people in need have they helped?

Average	1.04

7c. Do they still fight?

Yes	9

5b. What type of help have you offered?

Answer Provided	Responses
No answer	12
Need based help	5
Giving rice/vegetables	4
Giving advice	2
Giving Clothes	1
Giving Money	1

Rural Area Survey Snapshot

Literates

Sex	Persons
Male	12
Female	13

Age Range	19-42
Average Age	27

Knowledge

1. Who is Jesus?	
Answer Provided	Responses
Savior, God	14
God	8
Creator	3
no answer	0

3. Do they have Bible?	
Yes	25
No	0

Ability

4. Why is the Bible important?	
Answer Provided	Responses
Learn more about God	9
To grow spiritually	5
To know God's will	4
To live a better life	3
Word of God	2
Resist Devil	1
Way to our path	1

Experience

1. What was their life before accepting Christ?	
Answer Provided	Responses
Drunkard, smoking & dancing, fighting	11
Idol worshippers	10
Demon Possession	4
Worldly life	0

2. Why did they accept Jesus in to their life?	
Answer Provided	Responses
Because he is God	7
Healing	6
Through Gospel	6
To go to heaven	4
To live a holy life	1
No answer	1

3. What changes have taken place after accepting Christ?	
Answer Provided	Responses
Left Old bad habits	8
Got peace	8
Happy life & Fear of God	3
Family Saved	3
Miracle Happened	3

Behavior

1. How many people have they led to Christ?	
Average	**Responses**
1-2	14
3-4	4
above 5	5
No reply	2
Average	21

4. How do they respond when they were Hurt?	
Answer Provided	**Responses**
Forgive	11
Pray	7
No answer	3
Love	3
Fight Back	1
Leaving the place	0

5. How many people in need have they helped?	
Average	2.5

5b. What type of help have you offered?	
Answer Provided	**Responses**
Giving Money	8
Need based help	5
Giving rice/vegetables	5
No answer	3
Giving Clothes	2
Giving advice	2

6. What is their Daily Income	
Income (Rs.)	**No. of People**
0 - 50	7
Farmer	3
Evangelist	4
Housewives	9
Average Income	Rs. 39

6b. How much do they give to the church?	
Range	**No. of People**
1-5	3
6 - 10	2
11 & above	19
Average weekly contribution	15.7

7c. Do they still fight?	
Yes	2

Rural Area Survey Snapshot

Non-Literates

Sex	Persons
Male	9
Female	16

Age Range	19-45
Average Age	33

Knowledge

1. Who is Jesus?	
Answer Provided	**Responses**
God	14
Healer	3
Creator	2
Savior	1

Ability

3. Do they have Bible?	
Yes	19
No	6

4. Why is the Bible important?	
Answer Provided	**Responses**
Learn more about God	17
To grow spiritually	5
To know God's will	3
To live a better life	0
Word of God	0
Resist Devil	0
Way to our path	0

Experience

1. What was their life before accepting Christ?	
Answer Provided	**Responses**
Drunkard, smoking & witchcraft	10
Idol worshippers	7
Family Problems	4
Other bad habits	4

2. Why did they accept Jesus in to their life?	
Answer Provided	**Responses**
Healing	10
By observing Christians	6
Through someone	3
To get peace	2
To have eternal life	2
Solved problems	2

3. What changes have taken place after accepting Christ?	
Answer Provided	**Responses**
Left Old bad habits	10
Respectful life, Peace, Church	8
Loving and forgiving	5
Involved in ministry	1
Not much change	1

Behavior

1. How many people have they led to Christ?

Average	Responses
1-2	11
3-4	0
above 5	0
No reply	14
Average	0.8

4. How do they respond when they were Hurt?

Answer Provided	Responses
Keep quiet	11
Pray	7
Temptation to fight	3
Fight Back	3
Avoid	1
Leaving the place	0

5. How many people in need have they helped?

Average	0.04

5b. What type of help have you offered?

Answer Provided	Responses
No answer	15
Giving rice/vegetables	4
Giving Clothes	3
Need based help	2
Not in position to help	1
Giving Money	0

6. What is their Daily Income

Income (Rs.)	No. of People
0 - 50	16
Farmer	6
Evangelist	0
Housewives	3
Average Income	Rs. 34

6b. How much do they give to the church?

Range	No. of People
1-5	15
6 - 10	6
11 & above	4
Average weekly contribution	6.8

7c. Do they still fight?

Yes	5

Bibliography

Aiyar, Shankkar. "India's Worst." *India Today*, August 25, 2003.

Aiyar, Mani Shankkar. "India File: Poverty in China and India." *Washington Times*, January 1, 2003.

Andoor, Donald. "Group Identifies Illiteracy as Threat to Africa's Development." *This Day* (2002).

Babbie, Earl. *The Practice of Social Research*. 8th ed. Belmont, Ca: Wadsworth Publishing Company, 1998.

Bar-Ilan, Meir. "Illiteracy in the Land of Israel in the First Centuries C.E." *Essays in the Social Scientific Study of Judaism and Jewish Society*, II. New York: Ktav, 1992.

Barber, Stephen J. "Literacy as a Mission Tool to Reach Tribal Peoples." *International Journal of Frontier Missions* 15 (1998): 91–95.

Barclay, William. *Educational Ideals in the Ancient World*. Grand Rapids: Baker Book House, 1977.

Barrett, David B.; Kurian, George T.; Johnson, Todd M. *World Christian Encyclopedia: A Comparative Survey of Churches and Religions in the Modern World*. Vol. 1. 2 vols. Second ed. Oxford: Oxford University Press, 2001.

Barrett, David B.; Johnson, Todd M.; Crossing, Peter F. "Missionmetrics 2005: A Global Survey of World Missions." *International Bulletin of Missionary Research* 29, no. 1 (2005).

Bellamy, Carol. *The State of the World's Children 1999*, Education: United Nations Children's Fund, 1999.

Bilimoria, Purusottama. "Gandhi's Thoughts on Education in the Context of Religion." *Journal of Dharma* 9, no. October–December (1984): 353–373.

Bloomberg, Craig L. *Jesus and the Gospels: An Introduction and Survey*. Nashville: Broadman and Holman Publishers, 1997.

Bonhoeffer, Dietrich. *The Cost of Discipleship*. New York: The Macmillan Company, 1967.

Boomershine, Thomas E. "Jesus of Nazareth and the Watershed of Ancient Orality and Literacy." *Semeia* 65 (1994): 7–36.

Bosch, David J. *Transforming Mission: Paradigm Shifts in Theology of Mission.* Maryknoll: Orbis Books, 2000.

Boulton, Greg. "Orality, Literacy, and Rhetoric: Historical Transitions in Christian Communication." Master of Divinity, Emmanuel School of Divinity, 1995.

Brett, M. G. "Literacy and Domination: G. A. Herion's Sociology of History Writing." *Journal for the Study of the Old Testament,* no. 37 (1987): 15–39.

Brown, Colin, editor. *The New International Dictionary of New Testament Theology.* Vol. 1. 3 vols. Grand Rapids: Zondervan Publishing House, 1979.

Carnell, Corbin S. "A Rhetoric of Reading: C S Lewis's Defense of Western Literacy." *Christianity and Literature* 37, no. 2 (1988): 52.

Casley, D. J.; Lury D. A. *Data Collection in Developing Countries.* Oxford: Oxford University Press, 1987.

Census of India 1991, Part Iva—Social and Cultural Tables. 1991. Accessed. Available from http://www.censusindia.net.

Central Institute of Indian Languages. *Central Institute of Indian Languages, 1991.* Accessed 2004. Available from http://www.ciil.org/languages/indian.html.

Creswell, John W. *Research Design: Qualitative and Quantitative Approaches.* Thousand Oaks: Sage Publications, 1994.

Crouch, Andy. "The Emergent Mystique." *Christianity Today,* January 2004, 36.

D'Souza, Dilip. "Of White Powders and Other Benefits." *Rediff* (1999).

Douglass, Frederick. *Narrative of the Life of Frederick Douglass, an American Slave.* New York: Penguin Putnam, Inc., 1997.

Edman, V. Raymond. *The Light in Dark Ages.* Wheaton: Van Kampen Press, 1949.

Ellul, Jacques. *The Humiliation of the Word.* Translated by Joyce Main Hanks. Grand Rapids: William B. Eerdmans Publishing Co., 1985.

Faith in Action Study Bible: Living God's Word in a Changing World. Grand Rapids: The Zondervan Corporation, 2005.

Fast Facts: On Orality, Literacy and Chronological Bible Storying. 2005. Accessed. Available from http://www.chronologicalbiblestorying.come/articles/fast_facts.htm.

Fischer, Steven Roger. *A History of Reading Globalities,* ed. Jeremy Black. London: Reaktion Books LTD., 2003.

Gaebelein, Frank E. ed. *The Expositor's Bible Commentary.* Vol. 8. Grand Rapids: Zondervan Publishing House, 1984.

Gerhardsson, Birger. *Memory and Manuscript: Oral Tradition and Written*

Tradition in Rabbinic Judaism and Early Christianity: The Biblical Resource Series, ed. Astrid B. and Freedman Beck, David Noel. Grand Rapids: Wm. B. Eerdmans Publishing Company, 1998.

Goody, Jack, ed. *Literacy in Traditional Societies*. Cambridge: Cambridge University Press, 1968.

————. *The Interface between the Written and the Oral* (Studies in Literacy, Family, Culture and the State). Cambridge: Cambridge University Press, 1987. Reprint, 1999.

————. *The Power of the Written Tradition*. Washington & London: Smithsonian Institution Press, 2000.

Guralink, David B. ed. *Webster's New World Dictionary of the American Language*. New York: Simon and Schuster, 1982.

Harvey, John D. "Orality and Its Implications for Biblical Studies: Recapturing an Ancient Paradigm." *Journal of the Evangelical Theological Society* 45, no. 1 (2002): 99–109.

Hendriksen, William. *New Testament Commentary, Exposition of the Pastoral Epistles*. Grand Rapids: Baker Book House, 1978.

————. *New Testament Commentary, Exposition of the Gospel of Matthew*. Grand Rapids: Baker Book House, 1979.

Hensley, Rosemary. "Tia Eliza Says Yes: Literacy for the Least of These." *Other Side* 24, no. March (1988): 9.

Hillerbrand, Hans J. *The Reformation: A Narrative History Related by Contemporary Observers and Participants*. Grand Rapids: Baker Book House, 1978.

Hogg, W. Richey. "The Scriptures in the Christian World Mission : Three Historical Considerations." *Missiology* 12, no. October (1984): 389–404.

Hostetter, Paul E. "Literacy: A Fundamental Ministry." *Reformed Review* 19, no. March (1966): 16–17.

Human Development Report 1990. United Nations Development Programme, 1990.

India Census Data, 2001. 2001. Accessed. Available from http://www.censusindia.net/t_00_006.html.

Jaffee, Martin F. "A Rabbinic Ontology of the Written and Spoken Word: On Discipleship, Transformative Knowledge, and the Living Texts of Oral Torah." *Journal of the American Academy of Religion* (1967).

————. *Torah in the Mouth: Writing and Oral Tradition in Palestinian Judaism 200 BCE – 400 CE*. Oxford: University Press, 2001.

Jebasing, Emil. "Summary of the Proposals of the Follow-up Committee That Met on 27 Oct '05." *Bless India Gathering*. New Delhi, 2005.

Johnson, H. C. "Literacy and Revolution: The Pedagogy of Paolo Freire." *Worldview* 25 no.3, no. March (1982): 29–31.

Kalam, A. P. J. Abdul. *India 2020: A Vision for the New Millennium*. New Delhi: Penguin Books India, 2002.

Kamala, P. "Role of Adult Education in Rural Development: A Study in the Selected Villages of Two Districts in Tamil Nadu." Doctor of Philosophy, University of Madras, 1993.

Kelber, Werner H. *The Oral and the Written Gospel: The Hermeneutics of Speaking and Writing in the Synoptic Tradition, Mark, Paul and Q*. Philadelphia: Fortress Press, 1983.

Kennedy, Terry. "Literacy and Its Implications for the Church." *Eastern Journal of Practical Theology* 5, no. Fall (1991): 15–26.

Lal, Vinay. "Anti-Christian Violence in India, Manas." Accessed 2005. Available from http://www.sscnet.ucla.edu/southeastasia/index.html.

Lambert, Malcolm. "Heresy and Literacy, 1000–1530." *Journal of Ecclesiastical History* 47, no. April (1996): 342–343.

Latourette, Kenneth Scott. *A History of the Expansion of Christianity*. Vol. 1. 2 vols. New York: Harper and Row Publishers, 1970.

———. *A History of Christianity Volume 1: To A. D. 1500*. New York: Harper and Row Publishers, 1975.

———. *A History of Christianity Volume II: Reformation to the Present*. New York: Harper and Row, Publishers, 1975.

Laubach, Frank C. *India Shall Be Literate*. Fabri Press, 2007.

———. *The Silent Billion Speak*. New York: Friendship Press, 1945.

———. *Teaching the World to Read*. New York: Friendship Press, 1947.

———. "Literacy as Evangelism." *Foreign Missions Conference*, 16. Buck Hill Falls, PA: Committee on World Literacy and Christian Literature Foreign Missions Conference of North America, 1950.

———. *War of Amazing Love*. Westwood: Fleming H. Revell Company, 1965.

"Lausanne Occasional Paper No. 54, Making Disciples of Oral Learners." *Lausanne Committee for World Evangelization*. Pattaya, 2004.

Levine, Kenneth. *The Social Context of Literacy*. New York: Routledge and Kegan Paul Inc., 1986.

"Literacy: An Evolving Concept," *United Nations Literacy Decade 2003–2012*. United Nations, 2003. Accessed. Available from http://portal.unesco.org/education/ev.php?URL_ID=13206&URL_DO=DO.

Longenecker, Richard N., ed. *Patterns of Discipleship in the New Testament*. Edited by Richard N. Longenecker. Vol. 1, *McMaster New Testament Studies*.

Grand Rapids: William B. Eerdmans Publishing Company, 1996.

Lucien, Caleb Edouard. "The Relationship of Illiteracy to Spiritual Maturity." Master of Theology, Dallas Theological Seminary, 1989.

Man, John. *The Gutenberg Revolution: The Story of the Genius and an Invention That Changes the World*. London: Headline Book Publishing, 2002.

Mangalwadi, Vishal and Ruth. *The Legacy of William Carey*. Wheaton: Crossway Books, 1999.

Mason, David. *Reaching the Silent Billion: The Opportunity of Literacy Missions*. 190 vols. Grand Rapids: Zondervan Publishing House, 1967.

Massena. "The Impact of Literacy on the Haitian Protestant Churches—a Challenge for Actions and Reflection." Doctor of Ministry, Gordon-Conwell Theological Seminary, 2001.

McKinney, Carol V. "Culture Change and Its Relation to Literacy." *Missiology* IV, No.1, no. January (1976): 65–74.

McKnight, Scot. "Jesus Creed." *Christian Century* (2004).

Millard, Alan R. "The Question of Israelite Literacy: The Scribes Had Not Monopoly on Writing." *Bible Review* III, no. 3 (1987): 22–31.

Mofitt, Robert. "Transformation: Dream or Reality?" *Evangelical Missions Quarterly* 41, no. 4 (2005).

Montgomery, John Warwick, editor. *God's Inerrant Word: An International Symposium on the Trustworthiness of Scripture*. Minneapolis: Bethany Fellowship, Inc., 1974.

Moore, W. T. "Orality and Literacy: The Technologizing of the Word." *Christian Century* 100, no. March (1983): 285–286.

Murphy, David J. "The Word Became Flesh: The Importance of Orality for Mission in New Era." Master of Arts in Theology, Catholic Theological Union at Chicago, 1989.

"National Human Development Report 2001." *Delhi: Planning Commission Government of India*, March 2002.

Neff, David. "Where Would Civilization Be without Christianity?" *Christianity Today*, December 1999, 50–59.

Novak, Michael. "How Christianity Created Capitalism." *Religion and Liberty* 10, no. 33 (2000).

Olson, David R., and Nancy Torrance, eds. *Literacy and Orality*. New York: Press Syndicate of the University of Cambridge, 1991.

Olson, David R.; Nancy Torrance. *The Making of Literate Societies*. Malden: Blackwell Publishers Inc., 2001.

Ong, Walter J. *Orality and Literacy: The Technologizing of the Word New Accents*, ed.

Terrence Hawks. London: Metheun & Co. Ltd, 1982.

Pandjiris, G. "Literacy, Bible Reading and Church Growth through the Ages." *Missiology* 8, no. January (1980): 109–110.

Pettegree, Andrew. *The Reformation World*. London; New York: Routledge and Kegan Paul Inc., 2000.

Robinson, Andrew. *The Story of Writing*. London: Thames and Hudson Ltd., 2003.

Rogers, Cleon L. "The Great Commission." *Bibliothecra sacra* (1973).

Rycroft, W. Stanley and Clemmer, Myrtle M. *The Struggle against Illiteracy*. New York: Commission on Ecumenical Mission and Relations The United Presbyterian Church in the U. S. A., 1964.

Samra, James G. "A Biblical View of Discipleship." *Bibliothecra sacra* (2003).

Samuel, Vinay; Sugden, Christopher. "Transformation: The Church in Response to Human Need." *Consultation on the Church in Response to Human Need*. Wheaton, Illinois, 1983.

————. *The Church in Response to Human Need*. Grand Rapids: Wm. B. Eerdmans Publishing Co., 1987.

Samuel, Vinay, and Chris Sugden, eds. *Mission as Transformation*. Oxford: Regnum Books International, 1999.

Sanneh, Lamin. *Translating the Message: The Missionary Impact on Culture: The American Society of Missiology Series*. Maryknoll: Orbis Books, 1989.

————. *Encountering the West: Christianity and the Global Cultural Process: The African Dimension World Christian Theology Series*, ed. Reverend Dr Frank Whaling. Maryknoll: Orbis Books, 1993.

Schuyler, Joseph B. "Bemba Myth and Ritual: The Impact of Literacy on an Oral Culture." *Review of Religious Research* 29, no. September (1987): 85–86.

Sen, Amartya. *Development as Freedom*. New York: Anchor Books, 1999.

Shacklock, Floyd. *World Literacy Manual*. New York: The Committee on World Literacy and Christian Literature, 1967.

Shandilya, Tapan Kumar; Khan, Shakeel Ahmad. *Child Labor a Global Challenge*. New Delhi: Deep & Deep Publications (P) Ltd., 2003.

Siddhartha, Roy; Katoti, R. G. ed. *Statistical Outline of India 2004–2005*. Mumbai: Tata Services Limited, 2005.

Singh, K. S. *The Scheduled Tribes People of India National Series*, Vol. III. Delhi: Oxford University Press, 1994.

————. *India's Communities, People of India National Series*. Vol. VI. New Delhi: Oxford University Press, 1998.

Sivaswamy, G. "Top Priority Needed for Eradicating Illiteracy." *The Hindu*, September 11, 2001.

Slack, James. "What Specifically Is Chronological Bible Storying." *Exploring the Implications of Orality, Literacy and Chronological Bible Storying Concerning Global Evangelism*, 2001.

———. "Oral Memory and Its Implications Concerning Chronological Bible Storying." 3rd. 2004. Accessed 2005. http://www.newwway.org/articles/OralMemoryandImplication.pdf

Smith, Frank. "Unspeakable Acts Unnatural Practices: Flaws and Fallacies." *Scientific Reading Instruction*. Portsmouth: Heinemann, 2003.

Snyder, Arnold. "Orality, Literacy, and the Study of Anabaptism." *The Mennonite Quarterly Review* LXV, no. Number 4 (1991): 371–393.

Snyder, Howard A. *The Problem of Wine Skins*. Downers Grove: Inter-Varsity Press, 1975.

———. *The Radical Wesley and Patterns for Church Renewal*. Downers Grove: Inter-Varsity Press, 1980.

Stott, John R. W. *The Message of 2 Timothy: Guard the Gospel*. Downers Grove: Inter-Varsity Press, 1973.

———. *Christian Mission in a Modern World*. Downers Grove: Inter-Varsity Press, 1975.

———. *Involvement: Being a Responsible Christian in a Non-Christian Society*. Old Tappan: Fleming H. Revell Company, 1984.

Swanson, R. N. *Literacy, Heresy, History and Orthodoxy: Perspectives and Permutations for the Later Middle Ages*. Cambridge: Cambridge University Press, 1994.

Sweetland, Dennis M. *Our Journey with Jesus: Discipleship According to Luke-Acts*. Vol. 30 Good News Studies, ed. Robert J. Karris. Collegeville: The Liturgical Press, 1990.

Taber, Charles R. "In the Image of God: The Gospel and Human Rights." *International Bulletin of Missionary Research* (2002).

"The Lausanne Covenant." *Lausanne Committee for World Evangelization*. Lausanne: The Lausanne Commission, 1974.

"The Pattaya Statement." *Consultation on World Evangelism*. Pattaya, 1980.

Thomas, Jacob. *From Lausanne to Manila: Evangelical Social Thought*. Delhi: India Society for promoting Christian Knowledge, 2003.

UNESCO and Education, Paris: The Media Team Education Sector, UNESCO. Accessed. Available from *unesdoc*.unesco.org/images/0012/001289/128951e.pdf

UNESCO and Literacy: Strategy. 2005. Accessed. Available from http://portal.unesco.org/education/en.ev.php-URL_ID=41145&URL_DO=DO_TOPIC&U

UNESCO Millennium Development Goals (MGDs). 2005. Accessed http://portal.
   unesco.org/education/en.ev.php-URL_ID=41138&URL_DO=DO_
   TOPIC&U

"UNICEF Says India Must Improve Basic Education." *India Literacy Project,*
   December 8, 1998.

United Nations Literacy Decade (UNLD) and LIFE. 2005. Accessed http://portal.
   unesco.org/education/en.ev.php-URL_ID=41139&URL_DO=DO_
   TOPIC&U

Wadhwa, Soma. "When Numbers Lie." *Outlook India,* April 9, 2002.

Warfield, Benjamin Breckinridge. *The Inspiration and Authority of the Bible*
   Philadelphia: Presbyterian and Reformed, 1970.

Warren, Ruth Ure. *Literacy.* Christian Focus Pamphlets. London: Edinburgh
   House Press, 1955.

Watkins, Morris. *Literacy, Bible Reading, and Church Growth through the Ages.*
   Pasadena: William Carey Library, 1978.

Wesley, John. *The Works of John Wesley.* London: John Manson, 1829.

Wilkins, Michael J. *Discipleship in the Ancient World and Matthew's Gospel.* 2nd ed.
   Grand Rapids: Baker Book House Company, 1995.

Wilson, John D. "What It Takes to Reach People in Oral Cultures." *Evangelical
   Missions Quarterly* 27, no. 2 (1991): 154–158.

Winter, Ralph D.; Hawthorne, Stephen. *Perspectives on the World Christian
   Movement.* 3rd ed. Pasadena: William Carey Library, 1999.

Wright, Chris. "Re-Affirming Holistic Mission: A Cross-Centered Approach in
   All Areas of Life." *Lausanne World Pulse* 3.

Wright, N. T. *The New Testament and the People of God.* Minneapolis: Fortress
   Press, 1992.

Young, Ian M. "Israelite Literacy: Interpreting the Evidence Part I." *Vetus
   Testamentum* XLVIII, no. April (1998): 239–253.

———. "Israelite Literacy: Interpreting the Evidence Part II." *Vetus Testamentum*
   XLVIII, no. July (1998): 408–422.

Index